Inspired by Jonathan Reynolds' experience on location with Francis Ford Coppola and the crew filming **Apocalypse Now, Geniuses** takes us to the Philippine jungle, where genius director Milo McGee McGarr has been filming his war epic, **Parabola of Death**. After "three months in the worst country in the world," they've got only ten minutes of film in the can. And now a raging typhoon is about to hit.

While everyone else flees to Manila, four crew members remain stranded in a small house to wait out the storm. There's the screenwriter Jocko, a cynical East Coast intellectual whose biting humor centers mostly on California and on the voluptuous centerfold Skye Bullene, who's been flown in for a ten-second nude walk-on. Then there's the makeup man Bart, proud of the fact that he is known in the business as "Mr. Wounds," who resembles — and often thinks he **is** — "Papa" Hemingway. There's Winston, the Filipino

Rubbers were both extremely well received when they were produced at the American Place Theatre in 1975. His other plays include **Tunnel Fever**, written on a Rockefeller Grant for Playwriting, the book for the Manhattan Theatre Club revue *S͟t͟y͟n͟e͟* **After Styne** and the book f cal **Whoopee!** Mr. I of The London Academ matic Arts. One line of ken, by Robert Duvall, **lypse Now.**

GENIUSES

Jonathan Reynolds
GENIUSES

NELSON DOUBLEDAY, INC.
GARDEN CITY, NEW YORK

GENIUSES opened in New York on May 13, 1982 at
Playwrights Horizons, Paul Daniels Managing Director
and Andre Bishop Artistic Director. Direction was by
Gerald Gutierrez; sets by Andrew Jackness; lighting
by James F. Ingalls; costumes by Ann Emonts; sound by
Scott Lehrer; fights by B. H. Barry; special effects by
Esquire Jauchem and Gregory Meeh; production stage
manager J. Thomas Vivian. The cast, in order of
appearance, was as follows:

JOCKO PYLE	*Michael Gross*
SKYE BULLENE	*Joanne Camp*
WINSTON LEGAZPI	*Thomas Ikeda*
EUGENE WINTER	*David Rasche*
BART KEELY	*Kurt Knudson*
MILO MCGEE MCGARR	*David Garrison*

GENIUSES

CHARACTERS

WINSTON LEGAZPI. A slender, aesthetic-looking Filipino
boy-man, with a raft of children. Although he is a
professional bodyguard and expert with all sorts of
weaponry, at first meeting his occupation would seem
to involve poetry. He speaks excellent English, but
speaks it in phrases rather than sentences, as those
fluent in a second language often do.

SKYE BULLENE. Twenty-seven. An alumna of the *Playboy*
centerfold, and genuinely gorgeous in that
all-American, pixie-nosed, very blond sort of way. She
is aware of the impact her physique makes on others,
and it is her face and body that have determined her
varied career rather than any intellectual convictions.
She is a child of the suburbs, the product of an
attentive but middle-class family. She plays a guitar
and has been through most of the religions and drugs
inspired by California—though she is in no way
physically scarred by drugs. And she is full of surprises.

BART KEELY. He is in his mid-fifties, vigorous, athletic,
with an excellent physique. He consciously styles

himself after Ernest Hemingway and from a distance is a dead ringer for him. Bart is by turns funny, irascible, gentle, and brilliant, constantly going into and coming out of his own personal fog. The actor playing him must be able to make very fast transitions.

JOCKO PYLE. Mid-thirties. He is the only member of the crew from New York. A novelist who has yet to catch on, he is acidic, relentless, very funny, and angry, with a saving grace of self-deprecation.

EUGENE WINTER. Forty-two. Quiet, gentlemanly, and charming. He is the art director of *Parabola of Death*, and extremely good at his work. He is accustomed to enormous success and the pressure of swift and strict deadlines, and consequently he is more socially responsible and less eccentric than his counterparts from the lofts of New York might be—but he is, in every respect, an artist. He speaks quietly, sometimes even mumbling; but he is capable of sudden and violent rages, during which he becomes inarticulate.

MILO MCGEE MCGARR. At thirty-two, he has won six Oscars and is the current whiz kid of movie directors. He has an idea a minute, enormous energy and intelligence, and he delights in his own iconoclasm. He worked his way up from the slums of St. Louis, through film school, and, in addition to his artistic skill, which is considerable, he is a master con artist. He is short (ideally, but not essentially) and in every way has a style all his own.

ACT ONE

ACT ONE

The second story of a sturdy, attractive house in a small town two hundred miles north of Manila, the Philippines. A rich mahogany staircase leads downstairs near the Stage Left wall. A huge picture window is Upstage Center, behind which are thick, lush trees. The walls are of white stone and give the effect of an elegant building designed by Le Corbusier.

Four bedrooms and a bathroom surround a central area which contains (at least) a large, circular table, several chairs, and a dozen stacked cases of San Miguel, the local beer. Near the cases is a Polaroid camera. A light bulb hangs from a socket.

On a table against the wall stand several models of movie sets: a complete African village, a bamboo bridge surrounded by machine-gun emplacements, and a supply camp with miniature tanks and helicopters.

The rooms off the central area—five in all—are arranged like those in a French farce, though this configuration should not be emphasized. Two bedroom doors—Bart's and Eugene's—are Stage Left and Stage Right of the picture window, and a bathroom door is against the Stage Left wall. These rooms are revealed to us only when their doors are open.

A few feet Downstage of the bathroom door is the door to Skye's room; opposite Skye's room Stage Right is Jocko's room. These two rooms are constantly revealed to us, as one of their walls is our fourth wall. The sun flooding the space is glaring, heralding an approaching storm.

Several loud animal noises can be heard from Offstage —the cries of pigs, dogs, and chickens. It is very hot.

At rise, Jocko Pyle is sitting at his typewriter. He has just finished typing and is euphoric.

JOCKO: This is it! This is it! I've got it! "Exterior: Day. All is in flames. Overhead, the helicopters fire rockets, B-54s—or whatever they are—squirt napalm. Explosions and blood everywhere. Camera pans to reveal village littered with dead African bodies. Reverse on O'Hara. He is stunned, drops his M-16 and races to his lifelong friend, Lugumba, whose black African body is riddled with bullets, cradles his head in his arms." (*He breaks himself up with joy*) Milo, you're gonna love this, it's so great! I'm going to be the first person in history to win two Oscars for the same screenplay. (*Reading again from the paper*) "Lugumba whispers into O'Hara's ear. 'When this war is over, when the bombs have stopped and your fire-spitting birds have stilled their rotors, then you will come back to Angola.' O'Hara: 'Of course I will come back. Don't try to talk.' Lugumba: 'Then will we sip the sacred pooboo blood and we will run with the laughter of little children.' O'Hara: 'Yes, Lugumba.' Lugumba: 'For under our skins of coffee and vanilla we are—,' he gasps, 'brothers.' Lugumba's head falls to O'Hara's chest; he is dead. O'Hara shakes him wildly, tears streaming down his face. 'Lugumba, Lugumba!' Helicopters bank and break above, a new stream of napalm is fired in the background. Dolly back, revealing O'Hara wildly shaking Lugumba's black African body in the middle of this sea of charred humanity. We are in hell. Dissolve to the holocaust. The end." This is perhaps the most total piece of rubbish I have ever read. It gives new meaning to the expression "this sucks." If I had ever won an Oscar, they'd take it away from me for this. I can't do it. I can't do it. I just can't do it! I can't write, I never could write, I don't care if I get fired, Milo, go ahead, I can't do it, I can't do it! (*He takes a designer's tube and beats the typewriter. Then he furiously picks up the typewriter and mauls it. Suddenly the roller comes out of it*) Now, even if I *could* do it, I can't do it. (*He starts to exit*) I could do it if we had a few days, but there's no time!

(*Jocko exits into his room. Skye Bullene enters from her room and, overcome with a wave of nausea, exits into the bathroom. Winston Legazpi enters from downstairs carrying a tray with an ice bucket, glasses, and a bowl of calamansi fruit. He is singing, "New York, New York." He wears a* Parabola of Death *T-shirt. He sets*

his tray on the center table and clears away some
papers. Eugene Winter enters)

EUGENE: Winston! Winston! Hey, there you are. Let me
borrow your gun, my man. Just for a couple of minutes.

WINSTON: What? I cannot do that.

EUGENE: Oh, come on, come on, I'll be back in ten minutes.

WINSTON: But . . . why, Eugene?

EUGENE: I have to shoot the water buffalo.

WINSTON: What?

EUGENE: Listen. The scene we just shot, one of the water
buffalo tripped and broke his leg, and now it's got to be
killed.

WINSTON: Why . . . you?

EUGENE: No one else wants to do it. Look, you're my
bodyguard, aren't you? If I've got the gun, no Muslims
are gonna kidnap me.

WINSTON: No . . . I . . .

(Eugene steals the pistol from Winston)

EUGENE: Two shots! I'll pay you for them! Two bullets,
that's all! *(He exits with the pistol)*

WINSTON: Eugene! Eugene! My gun.

(*Skye enters from the bathroom on her way back to her room*)

WINSTON: Oh, . . . nice day.

SKYE: No it isn't.

(*Skye exits into her room. Bart Keely enters from the outside carrying a metal work box. He crosses down to the beer, opens one, drinks it; opens another, starts drinking that one. Winston fills a glass with ice. Bart picks up a bottle of vodka and pours the beer and vodka into the glass*)

BART: What's the art director doing with your gun?

WINSTON: He . . . has to kill the water buffalo.

BART: Oh, that poor water buffalo. That was terrible. Yeah, Eugene'd like that—killing a water buffalo. What's for supper?—never mind, don't tell me. Chicken and mango, chicken and mango. Chickens fall out of the sky in this place. This country has the scrawniest poultry I've ever seen. How do you kill 'em? Starve 'em to death?

WINSTON: I fix.

BART: Yeah, you fix.

(*Winston exits with tray. The noise outside increases*)

BART: Well, if it's gotta be chicken, I hope it's *that* one. Shut up out there! You! Pigs! Shut up! When the pigs get tired, out come the dogs. When the dogs get tired, out come the roosters! It's noisier out there than it is during the rush hour at Marrakech! Christ, it's hot.

(*Jocko enters with a screwdriver and pliers*)

JOCKO: Started without us, I see.

BART: Nothing the matter with that.

JOCKO: Bart, you can drink before *breakfast* if you want.

BART: This movie's never gonna get made. I don't care how many billions Milo McGee McGarr's made for those studios, this time, no sir. In my twenty-six years three months in this business I have never seen anything like it. The entire Philippine Air Force, three days of rehearsal, a thousand extras . . . they come to me for thirty-five gallons of blood! I stuck wounds on everybody, damn near ran out of latex. Special effects, explosions . . .

JOCKO: I know the sequence.

BART: . . . machine gun bullets, the best and the most that money can buy. Helicopters swooping down, huts blowing up, everything in flames, my blood spurting everywhere, extras running around screaming . . . six cameras! And after all that . . . not one foot of usable film! Because his Irish Highness, Milo McGee McGarr couldn't get the goddam Filipino helicopter pilots to fly into frame. Holy, holy, holy!

JOCKO: The whole shot was ruined? That means we're now . . . twenty-eight days behind schedule.

BART: What do you think that one shot coulda cost? Eighty-five thousand dollars? Ninety? Just to break even, this picture's gonna have to gross more than *Gone with the Wind, Star Wars,* and the two *Jawses* put together. As if anybody's gonna go see a movie about the war in Angola anyway.

JOCKO: This isn't a movie about the war in Angola, Bart— that's only the background. How many times do I have to tell you? This is a movie about a mercenary named O'Hara and his tormented struggle with a personal religion, the denial of a racial consciousness, and the discovery of his own sexual identity.

BART: I'd rather see a movie about the war in Angola. Come on, Monday it was about man's inhumanity to man. Tuesday it was about modern decadence or something, and last week it was about genocide, rock 'n' roll and T. S. Eliot.

JOCKO: Milo's very ambitious.

BART: This goddam script changes every day! I mean, I'm the make-up man, I just create the wounds and give out the blood—I don't need to know what the movie's about. But the writer! The director! And one more thing! You and Sir Milo might realize nobody's going to see a movie the title of which they can't even understand. *Parabola of Death.* I've had "parabola" explained to me sixteen times, and I still don't know what it means.

JOCKO: A parabola is a geometric curve, Bart—

BART: I know that! I don't have to be pandered to like a toad. But what does it mean?

JOCKO: Well, here "parabola"'s used to indicate the metaphysical connection between primitive innocence and man's love of killing . . .

BART: What're you gonna do—hand out dictionaries at the box office? Here we are, three months in the worst country in the world, two hundred miles from the worst city in the world, and only ten minutes of film in the can. Here, have a beer, boy.

JOCKO: No, no.

BART: Why not?

JOCKO: I don't like getting drunk in the afternoon.

BART: This isn't afternoon, this is evening—that's when you're supposed to get drunk. And who the hell gets drunk on one beer anymore?

(*Gunshots are heard*)

JOCKO: What was that?

BART: Eugene killing the water buffalo.

JOCKO: How awful. The poor thing. I hate guns. The water buffalo?

BART: Yeah. Wanna arm-wrestle?

JOCKO: No, Bart.

BART: Why not? Come on . . . you chicken?

(*Jocko leaves his typewriter and they get in position around the center table to arm-wrestle*)

JOCKO: Don't you ever get tired of this?

BART: Come on, come on.

(*Jocko and Bart arm-wrestle. Bart is much stronger and shows no effort. Jocko struggles and grabs hold of the table*)

BART: Leggo the table!

(*Jocko lets go of the table and Bart pins him quickly*)

BART: Awww, you weren't even trying.

JOCKO: I was too trying!

BART: Now the left hand.

JOCKO: Why the left hand?

BART: Hey, I'm right-handed. It's much harder for me.

JOCKO: Well, I'm right-handed too! It's much harder for me!

BART: Come on, come on. I won't make you suffer. (*They lock arms again. Bart takes his time, drinks his beer, and then pins Jocko again*) Beer's on me! Have a beer, boy.

JOCKO: No, I have to get back to work.

BART: What happened here?

JOCKO: I just beat up my typewriter.

BART: Don't get cute.

JOCKO: I did!

BART: I hate it when writers get cute. "I just beat up my typewriter." Just say what happened—it fell, I kicked it, it broke. Ho, I quake in living fear what you'll turn me into; years from now I'll pick up some trash novel of yours and you'll be making a ripe fool of some poor old man who just happens to look like Ernest Hemingway and making him say, "I just beat up my typewriter."

JOCKO: You *do* look like Ernest Hemingway.

BART: Everybody says that—that's not news. You should read a little Papa, you know that, Jocko boy? Sentimental maybe, but lean and to the point. "For an hour now the old man had been seeing the black spots and he was not afraid, for the fish was big and it was the most beautiful fish he had ever seen."

JOCKO: (*Typing*) Exterior: day. Dead bodies lie naked in the sun.

BART: No, no, good God, don't say that.

JOCKO: Why not?

BART: That's what got all those other writers fired—Morosini, Carvalho, all of 'em. Same thing.

(*Jocko rips the paper out of the typewriter*)

BART: I didn't mean you had to tear it up.

JOCKO: I don't want to get fired. I'm sick of being fired! I've been fired from every movie job I've ever had.

BART: How many's that?

JOCKO: Four—and this time it's gonna be different.

BART: Well, you can always go back to writing books. Isn't that why Milo hired you? For that best seller, *Pulleys* or something?

JOCKO: *Pulleys of Fear.* And it wasn't a best seller. It was just promising—voted most promising first novel by two hundred bookstores or something.

BART: *Pulleys of Fear. Pulleys of Fear. Pulleys of Fear.* That doesn't make any more sense than *Parabola of Death.*

JOCKO: But the people who read it, liked it. All five of them. At least they said they did. It was wonderful getting published—everybody I met wanted to know what I thought about everything. Women liked me. I fell in love twice.

BART: Well, one thing about books: you can't get fired from a novel.

JOCKO: Yeah, and there wasn't all this money, so many people you have to please. Just a little editor with glasses.

BART: Well, why don't you go back to it?

JOCKO: Know what you make as an author? Two books, six years, four thousand six hundred dollars. That's eight hundred sixteen dollars a year. You ever been laughed at by an IRS man? I should have known, nobody reports eight hundred dollars of taxable income. Except the oil companies, of course. What are you making on this? Scale?

BART: Scale? Are you nuts? Hey, this is *me* we're talkin' about, Jocko! You know who they call first for wounds? Me! Oh, they may call Dick Smith for age to make

Dustin Hoffman look one hundred and six in *Little Big Man,* or they may call what's-her-goddam-name who did Lee Remick up in *Jennie;* okay, they got age. But I got wounds. Some people even used to call me Mr. Wound! They don't talk minimum when they talk to me—didn't this time.

JOCKO: Mr. Wound?

BART: Are you kidding? Milo's going for the moon on this one. He got the best in each category from gaffer to A.D. This could be the greatest movie ever made—he's not going to staff it with a lot of second-raters. Ho, Milo McGee McGarr is the single best director alive and working today, and that's a promise. And you want to know why? Because he keeps things moving, that's why. No slow dollies with Bach on the soundtrack like the French, everybody spoutin' Commie politics. Haw, the French haven't made a dime on a movie worldwide since Bardot turned forty! You know why else? 'Cause Milo doesn't try to pull symbolism over your eyes. If a gun doesn't go off, it doesn't mean somebody's impotent or the crumbling of a civilization or some damn Italian thing. It's just a gun doesn't go off. And with Milo, no guy comes on with white make-up who's supposed to be death and sits around playing chess! Milo knows entertainment. Action. Y'know, like television. Scale. Mshgaw. The last time I even waved at scale was back in '67 with Sir Run-Run Shaw in Taiwan. Hoo, they kept me jumpin'! Sixteen, seventeen wounds a day—backstab gash, ankle crack, two flaming faces, blood by the gallon. They knew what they were doing. That was when I lived in California, before I moved to Hong Kong, back in the days when booze still ruled

the countryside. No goddam drugs and cocaine to con-
fuse everything.

JOCKO: Oh, booze is making a big comeback, Bart.

BART: It is?

JOCKO: Even in L.A. They're distressed by its lack of
mystique, but they're impressed you don't go to jail for
it and your nose doesn't fall off. (*Typing*) Exterior:
day, sunset.

BART: Hah, don't put that, we got three sunsets already.
That's what happens when you get a cameraman from
Ireland never seen a sunset. Three of 'em in the first
ten minutes. Look, just come up with an ending, Jocko
—that's why Milo hired you.

JOCKO: I've already come up with an ending—four of 'em.

BART: Although I don't frankly see why Milo's so con-
cerned about no ending. He's also got no beginning, no
middle, and no in-between. I mean look: either
O'Hara's got to die or O'Hara's got to live, right?
There's your ending. How about this? He lives . . . but
with a big wound.

(*Skye lurches out from her room and runs to the
bathroom*)

JOCKO: Hi.

(*Skye exits quickly into the bathroom*)

BART: Great looking, isn't she?

JOCKO: Yeah, but you know, even when actresses're deathly ill, they always know how to dress. It's not enough for her to *be* sick—she has to *dress* sick.

BART: How does she dress when she's healthy?

(*Jocko retrieves a centerfold photograph and opens it*)

JOCKO: Haven't you seen this? It's her Playmate centerfold. She was the Playmate of the Year a couple of years ago. Eugene had a bunch of these made up for her scene with O'Hara in the tent.

BART: (*Very impressed*) She's lovely. Has Eugene slept with her yet?

JOCKO: Hey, come on, she's only been here four days, and she's spent half of that in the bathroom. Eugene isn't Warren Beatty, you know.

BART: Poor kid, comes all the way over here, gets sick as a Filipino ferret for four days and for what? A thirty-second scene where everybody'll be staring at her naked breastelettos.

(*The toilet flushes. Skye enters, heading for her room*)

SKYE: I hate this country. You know? Oh, not the people of course. (*She exits into her room*)

BART: She's a lovely girl. Don't you think?

JOCKO: It's hard to admire someone whose chief concern in life is whether the Allman Brothers have grown as artists and human beings. Besides, constant nausea is a lousy aphrodisiac. And she's so coy. If this were another century, she'd have a fan.

BART: Come on now, be honest—you really would like to slip something between her sheets, wouldn't you? Come on, come on, be honest.

JOCKO: Be honest? She is beautiful, sexually magnetic, a small room for rent in the attic, but with so many lurid little secrets that would leak out over the years she'd keep me fascinated; clearly a command of all the physical fundamentals; with the tiniest hint of servility at the lips and a playful suspicion of cruelty around the eyes. She is wholly, infuriatingly desirable, and I would like nothing more from this bleak jungle experience than to lasciviate her head to toe with wet, drenching mouthplay.

BART: Wow, are you serious?

JOCKO: Yup! I mean every word. The only problem with her is: then what?

BART: Well, I won't stand in your way.

(*Eugene enters quickly, heads straight for his room, and says quite distinctly but still on the run*)

EUGENE: The movie's about to be canceled. (*He exits into his room. Bart and Jocko are stunned*)

JOCKO: What?

BART: What? What?

JOCKO: Hey, are you kidding? Eugene! Hey! Hey!

EUGENE: What?

JOCKO: Are you kidding? The movie's off? Are you serious?

BART: Jeehosophat!

EUGENE: (*Offstage*) That typhoon that was supposed to miss us didn't miss us. (*He enters*) It was just delayed. It's going to hit us square on the head tonight. It's gonna blow us right out of business.

BART: Yeah?

JOCKO: What do you mean? What's going to happen?

EUGENE: The army told Milo all my sets are gonna be destroyed.

JOCKO: What? All of them?

(*Eugene crosses to the models*)

EUGENE: Oh, the tanks are okay, and they've already got the helicopters inside, but what are they gonna do about my village? You can't protect an entire village from a typhoon. It'll be levelled. And who knows if the

bridge unit can stand up under all this? Goddammit!
(*He stomps off into his room*)

JOCKO: What's he so upset about? How bad can a rainstorm be?

BART: Rainstorm? Jesus, Jocko, for all your east-coast ed-
ucation, you're as dumb as a thick plank of cherry!
We've got a killer typhoon coming! It'll wipe out everything! Rain so hard it kills mice!

JOCKO: Vertical water that seeks out mice and kills them?

BART: It's been known to stun goats.

JOCKO: You mean we've got a mouse-killing, goat-stun-
ning typhoon on our hands?

BART: Don't get cute! This could last three, five, seventeen days! Just ask Winston. Winston! Bodyguard's
never around when you need him.

(*Eugene enters with suitcase. He starts to pack his
clothes*)

EUGENE: And you better get packed, too. The helicopter's
gonna be here any minute and you have to be on it.

JOCKO: Me?

BART: Me?

EUGENE: (*Indicating Jocko*) You.

JOCKO: Me. I knew it.

BART: What about me?

EUGENE: (*To Jocko*) Milo said you should pack everything you got. He's gonna be by in his helicopter to take us back to Manila. Winston! Winston! Here's your gun! (*He crosses to the top of the stairs and throws the pistol off*)

JOCKO: I knew it, I knew it! Everything I've got! What'd I tell you, Bart?

BART: What?

JOCKO: I've been fired.

BART: Maybe you're just going to Manila for a story conference.

JOCKO: You don't pack everything you've got to go to a story conference. You pack everything you've got 'cause you ain't comin' back.

(*Jocko exits into his room. Winston enters with his gun*)

WINSTON: Eugene—you said only two bullets . . . you use five. Five!

EUGENE: I got carried away. C'mon Jocko.

BART: Well what's supposed to happen to me? Am I gonna get left here all alone?

EUGENE: They'll come and get you when the typhoon's over.

JOCKO: (*Entering with bags*) I knew it, I knew it! It was so obvious.

BART: There's too much packing going on here! (*He exits into his room*)

WINSTON: Eugene!

EUGENE: Here, Winston, here's three hundred pesos. That's over eight dollars a bullet. Go buy yourself a bazooka! Now come on, hurry up!

(*Winston exits down the stairs*)

JOCKO: Jesus, is Milo going to fire me?

EUGENE: He didn't say he was.

JOCKO: I just can't face L.A. without a job.

EUGENE: Why don't you go back to New York?

JOCKO: You can't live in New York and expect to work in the movie business. There's no one to have lunch with.

EUGENE: (*Picking up sketch*) This is the first sketch I did of O'Hara's camp. Three years ago in March, right after Milo and I flew over here and talked to President Marcos about filming here. You know, Milo phoned me and said, "Eugene, I wanna do a war picture. The biggest ever. I wanna make warfare operatic." All he had was an idea and a title: *Parabola of Death*. Christ! Three years wiped out by a stupid storm.

JOCKO: God, Eugene, you and Milo are like Hitler and Albert Speer on this picture, you know that?

EUGENE: What's that supposed to mean?

JOCKO: Well, I've just never seen an art director with so much power.

EUGENE: Milo and I are a good team. That's why we win Oscars. But I'm sick of people saying Milo's like Hitler, you know? He's not.

JOCKO: No, no, I don't mean he has designs on Poland. I wonder if I should pack these typewriter ribbons or just leave them here for the natives to eat.

EUGENE: How's whatshername?

JOCKO: Sick as a Filipino ferret, whatever that means.

EUGENE: Too bad the typhoon couldn't wait until she was well enough to make a pass at.

JOCKO: That what you had in mind?

EUGENE: I love women, Jocko. I mean, I love women, but right now I want them all to die. All of them just to drop dead.

JOCKO: Okay. (*He exits into his room*)

EUGENE: Come on, you done?

JOCKO: (*Offstage*) No, I have to pack everything I've got, remember?

EUGENE: Well, Milo's going to be here in a couple of minutes.

(*Bart enters with two suitcases*)

BART: Well, I'm packed.

EUGENE: Bart, you're not going. There's no room . . . in the helicopter.

BART: Well, who all's going?

EUGENE: Milo, me, Jocko, and Winston.

BART: Winston! You mean you get the bodyguard? What if something happens to us?

JOCKO: (*Entering*) Bart, I doubt the Muslims are gonna come all the way up from Mindanao in the middle of a typhoon. It's seven hundred miles away. (*He exits into his room*)

BART: Well . . . what's everybody else going to do?

EUGENE: Everybody else is gonna sit out the typhoon up here.

JOCKO: (*Entering*) You'll be all alone with the Playmate of the Year, Bart. Creamy expansive thighs, multi-colored underwear . . .

BART: Drop dead, mister. I've got my Miriam, and that's more than any five men can handle.

(*Skye enters combing her hair. No one sees her. She crosses up to the window and looks out; turns and speaks*)

SKYE: Man, I had a dog . . . died on a night like this.

BART: What? A dog?

SKYE: ~~Oh yeah~~, I've had dogs all my life. ~~Hi, Eugene~~. I'd just been to my prom, ~~my senior prom,~~ my Pismo Beach senior prom—maybe the last of its kind in a dying America.

BART: Your prom?

SKYE: ~~Oh~~ yeah, like Pismo Beach was famous for its proms. We were always on the news. The gym was all decorated; ~~we had a sixteen-piece band~~. We had a theme and everything. You know how other proms have themes like "Buttons and Bows," and "Spring Is For Lovers"? Not Pismo Beach. My year the theme was "The Meaning Of Life." Heavy, huh? Steve had just picked me up in his Chevy. He was cute, Steve, but he wasn't . . . neat, you know?

(*The three men abruptly exit into each of their rooms respectively*)

SKYE: Hey, what's going on here?

EUGENE: (*Entering with suitcase*) Jocko and I have to go back to Manila. Just for a couple of days. There's a typhoon coming.

SKYE: A typhoon?

EUGENE: Don't worry, it's only for a couple of days. You'll be perfectly safe.

(*Bart enters with vodka and beer*)

EUGENE: Bart'll be here to protect you.

SKYE: Bart? (*She looks him over*) I guess it'll be okay.

JOCKO: It better be okay—you haven't got any choice.

SKYE: You going too?

JOCKO: No, I always throw my clothes around the room before a typhoon. Something my folks taught me. (*He folds a sweater*)

SKYE: You brought a sweater over here? Gee, I wouldn't have thought there'd be much use for a sweater in all this jungle heat and humidity. Oh, and hey, look! He brought a suit.

JOCKO: Why don't you just go over there and tell everybody about your dead dog.

SKYE: Hey, don't badmouth my dog, man.

JOCKO: What was the little dear's name?

SKYE: Oh, he had tons. *of names* His real name was Mr. Poochie, but soon everybody was giving him names. Joyce called him "P" for Pooch, Tenille called him Doctor Sir Poochie Dan. Then there was All Pooched Up And No Place To Go . . .

BART: All those were his names? What a dog tag!

SKYE: . . . the Get-Down Pooch, Mr. Dog, C-A-T Cat . . .

JOCKO: So when it died, it must have killed you.

SKYE: Oh, when he died it killed me. It was on a night like this—you know, about to rain and everything. I just got back from the prom, and some pre-teen boys came along outside our house and set him on fire with a Zippo—remember Zippos? It was awful.

BART: My God! Set him on fire! What did you do?

SKYE: Oh, I had a real mystical experience about it.

JOCKO: A real mystical experience about a dead dog . . . Have you, by any chance, done EST?

SKYE: Are you kidding? EST, TM, primal screaming, actualization. I got my Camaro through chanting and my

name through numerology. You don't get christened
Skye Bullene, you know. It comes from before. If it's
been worshipped, I've done it. But I'm way beyond all
that religious shopping now; my new old man is the
discoverer of Wattage Therapy—Dr. Sonny Latesco
Hiln.

JOCKO: Wattage Therapy? What's that?

SKYE: Oh, man, don't you read *Time* magazine? Wattage
Therapy is like a scientifically emotional, quasi-
confrontational behavior interaction with like a reality-
oriented, verbal parry-thrust system to protect the
waking psyche from emotion-whittling guilt attacks.

JOCKO: What?

SKYE: Oh yeah. It's universal. People are filled with love,
but they try to cut you down. So Dr. Sonny devised
systems to counter these cut-downs more efficaciously
than ever before in history. And Dr. Sonny has called
these systems verbal harmies, verbal tauntlets, acute
verbal harmies, simple verbal harmies once removed,
and et cetera.

JOCKO: Do me a favor—don't go on.

SKYE: Why not?

JOCKO: Skye, isn't it true that beneath all your verbal harmies and secondarily related tauntlets, the funda-
mental belief of Wattage Therapy and Dr. Sonny Late-

sco Hiln is that you and you alone are the center of the universe?

SKYE: Every human being is the center of his or her own universe. I am the center of mine. You are the center of yours.

JOCKO: I am not. I know this is heresy, but I actually believe there are some things in the world more important than me. Look at this woman, Bart—this is the Los Angeles contribution to twentieth-century America: competitive self-absorption.

SKYE: Hey, what is this? I'm just a poor, dazed, sick actress, and suddenly I'm getting jumped all over by some east-coast L.A.-hater.

JOCKO: I don't hate L.A.—where the smog creeps in on little rat feet. I love L.A.! City of Sculptable Air! Land of the Marshmallow Syntax! Home of the Richard M. Nixon Freeway!

BART: They got a freeway named after him?

JOCKO: Yup. Runs for just over a mile. They abandoned it when he started to look bad. That's the way L.A. deals with everything: lose a little popularity, they cut off your freeway.

SKYE: New York isn't the only city in the world with a ballet company, you know.

JOCKO: Yeah, but in L.A., the prima ballerina is still Esther Williams.

SKYE: Boy are you sour. It's not my fault everybody wants our kind of life and practically nobody wants yours. All those neckties and overcoats and tweeds. Whoopee—the seasons change! Why do you think all movies and television are done in Los Angeles? Not only because we do it better but 'cause we know exactly what the American people want! And we give it to them!

JOCKO: Oh, really?

SKYE: And don't give me a lot of superiority about how all the books and magazines are published in New York. Why do you think they're written in the first place?

JOCKO: Why?

SKYE: To get made into movies and television!

JOCKO: I fall to my knees in wonder.

SKYE: The shifting of the entertainment industry from New York to Los Angeles is the single most significant event in America in the last twenty-five years—something you've never gotten over. That and the fact that trend-starting has moved to the west coast.

JOCKO: Trend-starting? Is that a profession now?

SKYE: You know what I think? I think that whilst this fellow here has heard of Los Angeles, Los Angeles has never heard of him.

JOCKO: Very perceptive. And you know what I think? I think we are in the presence of a profound chowderhead.

SKYE: Hey!

JOCKO: She is an unemployable, narcissistic dilettante with no interests in life but the self-involved.

SKYE: What do you mean?—I'm perfectly employable. I'm an actress!

JOCKO: Oh, an actress! And what does that mean? You go to an acting class run by some old man father-figure who once knew Marilyn Monroe. He gets you to cry your eyes out over some boring childhood memory, and bingo—you're an actress! Never learn how to act another character, just polish up your own psychoses and present them to the public. That's not acting, Skye honey, that's emotional exhibitionism.

SKYE: I don't have to justify myself to you. I am a serious and dedicated actress.

JOCKO: So serious and dedicated, your daily fencing and voice lessons have developed an instrument of such discipline you have no trouble following a matinee of *Yeoman of the Guard* with an evening as Saint Joan; possessor of such a mature emotional range, you can tackle both the daffy ingenue and Madame Ranevskaya with aplomb; a consummate student of speech rhythms able to leap from Shakespeare to Congreve to Shaw, all in the same week of repertory. That serious and dedicated?

SKYE: But I don't want to do all that!

JOCKO: Of course you don't—that's the problem! You haven't a single artistic aspiration in your body! The only thing you west-coast cheerleaders ever aspire to is the complete and total display of your boring and unimaginative emotions.

SKYE: My emotions are not boring! They're shattering! Everybody says so!

JOCKO: Emotions are *always* boring except to the person having them. And what makes you think yours are different from anyone else's? You're sad, you're happy, you're angry, you're not, you're lonely, you're in love— who isn't?

SKYE: Well, what, in your twisted New York garbage-strike view of life, is so important if emotions aren't?

JOCKO: What you do, not what you feel. Accomplishments! That's what you're measured by in the world and that's what you should be measured by, but it's a hell of a lot harder to accomplish anything than it is to sit around wallowing in your own psychological entrails!

SKYE: Oh, and what am I supposed to do about it?

JOCKO: Get out of your twenties for a start. I'm sick of people in their twenties all trying to find themselves and inflicting their monumentally insignificant little

discoveries on everyone else. We know this already!
Why can't you all just go find yourselves at home,
quietly, behind closed doors—and then, when you're
thirty, come out and I'll buy you a drink.

SKYE: Oh, that's just a trick answer. And what great accomplishments have you ever pulled off? I know about
you—two dumb books nobody's ever heard of, fired
from every movie job you've ever had! What great accomplishments have you ever pulled off?

JOCKO: None! Don't you think I know that? I haven't accomplished a single thing in my life—and it makes me
depressed, crazy, suicidal! I've been living on the bor-
der of self-strangulation every minute of my last fifteen
years! But at least I *know* I haven't accomplished anything; at least I'm not a useless slug pretending that
her insatiable self-indulgence is actually of benefit to
somebody.

BART: Oh, come on, Jocko, she's a lovely girl. Just take a
look at her.

JOCKO: You take a look at her, Bart. Go ahead—she wants
you to. She has wonderful breasts that cry to be fon-
dled, a tantalizing Episcopalian nose that's made our
country great, fleshy thighs to warm your hips, the soft
sweet countenance of a cherub aloft, eh? Well, I'll
wager you this woman here knows every erotic line ever
attempted in the Western Hemisphere by man,
woman, or child and succumbed to ninety-eight per-
cent of them. Am I right?

SKYE: That's none of your business. And what are you—the Filipino branch of Moral Majority? You're a real conservative, aren't you?

JOCKO: I've never been a conservative. I used to be a Marxist—belonged to a Marxist club and everything.

BART: What happened?

JOCKO: All the other members were millionaires and wouldn't talk to me. But tell me, Skye, honey: when did you grow breasts?

SKYE: What?

EUGENE: You don't have to answer.

SKYE: I know. June of '65. I was eleven and a half.

JOCKO: Somehow I just knew you'd know the date. Tell me one more thing, Skye. What was the most number of people you slept with in one day?

SKYE: You really want to know? You sure? On a teeming July afternoon in '78, I once got it on with three different dudes in three different houses. And it was sensational—a sucking and flowing you'll never experience in your uptight, bottled-up life. The only difficulty there was the commute.

JOCKO: But I bet you've got control when you want it . . .

SKYE: Oh, I once didn't have relations for nine months running—that's how much control I've got.

JOCKO: That's the important part, Bart. She's not just promiscuous—

SKYE: God, no! I've got friends who are promiscuous—

JOCKO: She's got control over it. Copulating's only half her arsenal.

BART: What's the other half?

JOCKO: Not copulating! This is sexual politics, Bart, not equal pay for equal work. Look at her, Bart, a golden girl, somnambulant with a headline knowledge of the world—

BART: That may be going too far.

JOCKO: —vacuous, vaginal, fraudulent, hypocritical, a violent narcissist, an emotional onanist! Unremarkable except for a few biological features and an exuberant ordinariness—

BART: Oh, Jocko, no!

JOCKO: —grasping and desperate, she is the wretched epitome of the unthinking and the unthoughtful, a walking, marginally lifelike shrine to antithought. She isn't fit to cream your calloused feet.

BART: Well, maybe you're right.

JOCKO: And you wonder why I hate this creature more than life itself!

(*Pause*)

EUGENE: I'm exhausted.

(*There is a pause. KA-BOOM! Lightning and a thunderclap—it shakes the house. Incredible wind and rain flies in the windows. All windows and doors fly open*)

EUGENE: What the hell was that?

BART: Get your windows! Close your windows! Hurry! Hurry!

(*They all run and close their windows. The scene is chaotic*)

JOCKO: (*Entering*) Should we barricade the windows?

BART: (*Offstage*) No, just close them!

(*Another thunderclap frightens Jocko. He exits into his room. Skye enters*)

SKYE: What do I do? What do I do?

BART: (*Entering*) Help her, Eugene.

(*Eugene enters, and he and Skye exit into her room*)

BART: Winston! Winston!

(*Winston enters drenched. Jocko re-enters, and the three men struggle at closing the windows*)

JOCKO: Christ, I've never seen anything like this!

BART: I told you, didn't I?

(*They finally get the windows closed. They are all soaked. The walkie-talkie beeps. Jocko rushes to it*)

JOCKO: It must be Milo. Go ahead, go ahead, over! It's raining!

(*Eugene rushes in and grabs the walkie-talkie*)

EUGENE: Give me that! (*He speaks into the walkie-talkie*) This is Eugene, over!

(*Milo's voice, distorted but clear, is heard over the walkie-talkie*)

MILO'S VOICE: This is Milo. We're coming in for a landing, over!

JOCKO: Coming in for a landing? Is he crazy?

EUGENE: Hold it, Milo, hold it! There's a typhoon out there, over! Can you see him?

BART: Christ no, can't see a thing! Black as rain out there.

SKYE: Is he going to make it?

JOCKO: He can't make it!

SKYE: Go back, Milo, go back.

JOCKO: This is awful!

WINSTON: Oh, no, Mr. McGarr!

MILO'S VOICE: Too soupy down there. Can't do it. We've got to go back to Manila, Eugene, over.

EUGENE: But what about us? Over.

MILO'S VOICE: I'll get you outta there, Eugene! We'll finish it! I swear by the Academy of Motion Picture Arts and Sciences I will finish this picture! Over and out.

EUGENE: Jesus! The future of the whole picture's down in Manila, and I'm stuck up here. (*He picks up a can and pounds it several times on the table. Everyone stops to watch him. He notices their stares and stops*) Get me a calamansi juice, Winston!

WINSTON: Yes, Eugene. (*He exits*)

BART: Have a beer.

EUGENE: I don't drink.

JOCKO: Well, I do. Look, this'll have to go on for a few days at least, won't it? I mean really.

BART: Wanna arm wrestle?
JOCKO: No, Bart.
BART: Why not? Come on.... you chicken?

SKYE: I know all everybody wants to do is lay me, but what'm
I supposed to do? If I make it with one of you, the other two'll
just get pissed off, and then it's all over.
EUGENE: Is that the only reason we haven't made it? 'Cause you
think it'll piss off them?
SKYE: Of course. This is very political.

SKYE: I really feel good about myself, you know?…
No, like really. I mean like I make a living. I have dimensional,
non-suffocating relationships. Hobbies.
JOCKO: Now, there's a nice grown-up word, isn't it? Hobbies.

SKYE: Look at this face! You think I'd give up my one crack at revenge for what you just offered me? Unh-unh!

BART: Oh, at least.

JOCKO: Maybe a week! I can write six screenplays, two novels, and a *New Yorker* profile in a whole week! I can't wait until tomorrow so I can start my rewrites.

BART: Why don't you start now. Won't bother us.

JOCKO: No, I can't get to sleep if I write at night. John Cheever has the same problem. Hey, are we going to be okay here?

BART: Sure, we got everything we'll ever need. All kinds a' supplies; beer, calamansi . . . We can outlast any goddam typhoon these Filipinos want to throw at us.

JOCKO: Ah, calamansi—the perfect Filipino fruit. Just like this country; can't make up its mind whether it wants to be an orange, a lemon, or a lime. The millions of overpopulated and underemployed Filipinos are so busy squeezing these things into juice, they haven't got time for a revolution.

SKYE: Don't you ever talk to me like that again. And another thing; That was a pretty good try, Muldoon, but nobody but nobody gets into these pants unless and until I say so! (*She exits into her room*)

EUGENE: And they're so tiny . . . Tinier than the moon.

CURTAIN

ACT TWO

ACT TWO

Four days later.

It is night. The rain and wind are ferocious outside. There is no electricity.

As the house goes to black, everyone but Winston enters with trays of candles. They are placed on the up center table, the right table, the down right table, the center table, and on the stage floor down left. One candle is placed on top of the beer crates and one kerosene lamp is placed on the up center table.

Eugene is sitting in the down left chair carving a candle with Skye at his feet painting his toenails with polish, which we do not see. Jocko is writing at the center table and Bart is standing in his doorway, slamming the door without success. They are all in various stages of drunkenness, except Eugene.

BART: Nothing in this country works. (*He slams the door. It pops open*) Rain won't stop, doors won't shut.

(*Slam*) The grease on precision instruments is too thick for the instruments to be precise. (*Slam*) Perfect earth for coffee beans here, and they drink nothing but Nescafe. (*Slam*) Three and a half centuries of Spain, fifty-five years of us, and they haven't learned anything but disco music and T-shirts. (*Slam*) People are too short to matter much. (*Slam*) And then there's Tagalog . . .

JOCKO: Mluck mluck!

EUGENE: Bong bong dito!

SKYE: Mullow mulock blong!

(*They continue the Tagalog*)

BART: Mauwwrrgghhh! (*He slams the door one more time. It pops open again*) I'm going to bed.

SKYE: Okay. Finished.

(*Skye moves away and Eugene stands up, showing us his painted toenails. Skye shines a flashlight on them. Eugene walks around posing*)

EUGENE: How do I look?

SKYE: I think they're fabulous.

JOCKO: Come and see Eugene and his flaming feet!

EUGENE: Give me your pesos, Yankee, give me your pesos!

BART: This is sick.

SKYE: Oh, you look fabulous!

(*Eugene glides into tai-chi exercises. Jocko writes silently. Bart looks around restlessly*)

BART: Goddammit, I hate these eggs! (*He cracks open a raw egg and gulps it down*)

JOCKO: One thing I'll give L.A., boy. You've got the best hot fudge sundae in North America. I'm not talking Switzerland now, I'm not talking the Sacher Hotel, I'm not even talking Cadbury's Fruit and Nut Bar. Just hot fudge and just North America.

SKYE: I have a friend who says the best restaurant in America is in Kansas City.

JOCKO: Kansas City? Your friend is a gibbon.

BART: Is this important? This isn't important. This is duller than televised golf.

(*They lapse into silence. Eugene performs push-ups. Bart notices something on his back and runs to get the Polaroid camera. He snaps pictures of Eugene's back*)

EUGENE: What are you doing?

BART: You've got the most incredible scars. Can hardly see them. You don't mind, do you? I keep a notebook of scars.

EUGENE: I don't care.

BART: They look like razor blades. Who gave 'em to you?

EUGENE: My wife.

SKYE: You've been married?

EUGENE: Yup—in a church and everything. I fainted.

JOCKO: You fainted at your own wedding? How come?

EUGENE: It wasn't the heat. That's enough, Bart. And knock off the questions.

(*Bart sits down, Eugene puts on his shirt, Jocko writes. After a pause*)

JOCKO: Got one for you.

BART: Oh, Christ, not again.

SKYE: Another limerick?

BART: Well, it better be better than "The Bulldog Named Ike." I don't want to have to go through that one again.

SKYE: Oh, go on, Jocko, go on—I love your limericks.

BART: Yeah, yeah, go ahead, bore us to tears, tire us out beyond redemption . . .

JOCKO: Sorry, Bart. "On Venus They Practice Fella-
tio" . . .

> On Venus they practice fellatio
> Employing a six to one ratio.
> A tangle of toes,
> Sixteen eyes and a nose,
> And on one leg a very strange space shoe.

BART: Bwahh! Space shoe, space shoe, that's terrible! Are
you kidding?

SKYE: I thought it was wonderful! You really are a genius
when it comes to limericks, you know that, Jocko?

JOCKO: I had an agent on the coast who said I was a genius. Of course, everybody's a genius in the movie business. Right after they serve you the obligatory white
wine: "Jocko, we've read your book, and we here at
ICM think you're a genius." Einstein, Stravinsky, Balan-
chine—and me.

BART: Go on, go on. Stravinsky was no genius, and space
shoe is a lousy rhyme for ratio.

SKYE: I've got a limerick.

EUGENE: You wrote a limerick?

SKYE: Well, no, it's an old one I just remembered when
Jocko was doing all of his yesterday. Okay?

BART: Well, let's hear it!

SKYE: Okay. I hope you like it.
    O Britain, O Britain, land of the free,
    Home's where the heart is, and my heart's with thee.
    O Britain, Great Britain, land of the free,
    O Britain, *my* Britain, you're first rate with me.

(*After a pause*)

BART: That's lovely, dear.

JOCKO: That's not a limerick.

SKYE: Why not?

JOCKO: Doesn't have the right number of lines, the right number of syllables, the right emphasis, nothing. You didn't even get the rhyme scheme right: it's supposed to be AABBA. Yours was AAAA. And subcretinous.

SKYE: Oh, you're always intellectualizing, Jocko. Then what was it?

JOCKO: It was a . . . I don't know what it was, it was so terrible. Your limerick was to limericks what Filipino food is to food.

BART: (*Unfolding crumpled paper*) Oh well, here we go, Mr. Limerick—I've got it! You think that was bad—and it was—wait'll you hear this one. "The Bulldog Named Ike." By Jocko Pyle . . .
    At Christmas a bulldog named Ike
    Loved to sing Sapphic songs in a mike.

Ike became so obsessive,
His glands so aggressive,
By June he'd turned into a dyke.
I love it! I love it! It's so terrible! Peeee-yoooo! How
can a male bulldog turn into a female dyke! You
missed a whole surgical step! It wasn't even dirty.

JOCKO: One of the unfortunate consequences of a typhoon—the make-up man thinks he's Edmund Wilson.

BART: Well, if you'd rather waste your life writing limericks, why don't you just give us another limerick?

JOCKO: I just gave you two.

BART: I wouldn't call that much of an *oeuvre*. Well, limericks are too dainty for me, too much like doilies. I like
rougher earth: jokes.

JOCKO: Shoot. Give us a joke, Bart.

BART: Oh, no!

JOCKO: Why not?

BART: Are you kiddin'? You'd deliberately not laugh and
humiliate me till I was blue in the face.

JOCKO: No, we wouldn't. Really.

EUGENE: Of course we wouldn't.

BART: If there's one thing I can't stand, it's humiliation.

JOCKO: Now, come on, Bart. Give us one.

BART: I wouldn't give you a joke if you were the last man on earth and he was a Filipino.

JOCKO: I don't quite know what that means, but come on, give us a joke. Or was that a joke?

BART: No, no—you'll recognize my jokes when you see them. (*Pause*) For instance, you know how to get an elephant into a cigarette pack?

JOCKO: How?

BART: Take out twenty camels.

SKYE: Hey, hey, that's kind of funny.

BART: Oh, I got a million of 'em. Y'see—no sissy limericks for me. Do you know how the Lone Ranger gets rid of his garbage?

SKYE: Te-dah-dump, te-dah-dump, te-dah-dump-dump-dump. Do you know the story of the cross-eyed teacher? She could never control her pupils. You're not laughing, Jocko.

JOCKO: I'm laughing on the inside, Bart.

BART: Goddammit! You want prejudice? I can give you that, too! What did Abraham Lincoln say after a three-day drunk? —I freed who? (*Pause*) You know what the president of Harvard said to a student's father? —I got some bad news and some good news. The bad news is your son's a fruit; the good news is he's homecoming queen! You son of a bitch, just knock off this goddam game or you'll wreck the place!

(*Bart grabs two eggs from the bowl and throws them at Jocko, one at a time. He misses Jocko but hits the formerly white wall. Eugene cleans it up*)

EUGENE: Jesus, Bart!

BART: Well, I had to, or he'd wreck the place.

JOCKO: I was laughing, Bart. I was laughing.

BART: That's not a laugh—think I don't know that? You just take an old man (who happens to look like who I happen to look like) and force him to the farthest tangent on his circle—set him up for one of your godless, nihilist short stories. It's not my fault we're trapped here like rats in a trap! No food, no water, four days without no rain. Electricity all shot. If it hadn't been for me there wouldn't be any candles! Stronger men than us have buckled under conditions like these. Nothing but vodka and beer, vodka and beer . . .

JOCKO: You don't have to drink the vodka, Bart. And I don't write short stories.

BART: Oh, not good enough for you, eh? Well, you don't write movie scripts either. You haven't done lick one of work since this rain started. Milo can always replace you, y'know!

JOCKO: Whatta you mean? I put in three hours Wednesday, four hours on Thursday, six hours yesterday, two hours today . . .

BART: Two hours! Four hours! Who the hell works two and four hours a day! What kind of welfare job is that?

JOCKO: Most writers don't work more than four hours a day.

BART: Ernest Fernando Hemingway wrote six and seven and eight hours a day! And he wrote standing up! You wanna arm-wrestle?

JOCKO: No, Bart, I'm busy.

BART: Then just watch it!

(*They stew for a moment. Winston enters dressed in a yellow slicker and hat. He is soaking wet*)

EUGENE: Winston!

WINSTON: Excuse me, Eugene, I . . . have some food . . . from next door . . . good and hot!

BART: Hot?

WINSTON: Yes, Bart. Barney Roxas next door . . . has one gas cylinder. He heat it up . . . gave me a pot. It's meat.

BART: Yahoo!

SKYE: Meat! Oh, my God, fantastic! What kind of meat?

WINSTON: Dog.

SKYE: Dog?

BART: Yippee! Bring it on up, Winston!

EUGENE: Yes, bring it on, Winston!

SKYE: Wait a minute, Winston! You're really going to eat a dog? A little dog?

BART: It's delicious! A Filipino specialty!

SKYE: Puppy dog?

WINSTON: About this big.

BART: You'll love it.

JOCKO: Love it.

SKYE: I can't eat a dog!

BART: Why not?

SKYE: What kind is it?

WINSTON: I don't know.

SKYE: I would never eat a dog. The thought is revolting!

JOCKO: Then don't. Let us eat the cute little bowzer.

SKYE: How can you?

BART: Oh, for Chrissake, you pansy, it's delicious!

EUGENE: It's very good, Skye. Why don't you just try it?

SKYE: Ung-*unh*.

JOCKO: It comes in a pot, you know, like a stew. It's not all laid out like a poodle with a cute little designer raincoat. You won't even recognize it.

SKYE: No way. No dog. Aren't there any vegetables, Winston?

JOCKO: There's a typhoon going on outside! What's he supposed to do, go pick broccoli for you in the middle of a typhoon? Besides, you'd spend the next three days in the bathroom.

WINSTON: Uh . . . yes?

EUGENE: Sure. We're starving.

(*Winston exits*)

JOCKO: I was once offered a filet of cocker spaniel, but I turned it down flat.

BART: Filet of cocker spaniel! Are you kidding? You know where that dog comes from? The street. There's probably nine breeds in that thing we're going to eat. Filet of cocker spaniel—what do you think this is, Elizabeth Barrett Browning's? Think we're gonna eat Flush?

JOCKO: Your range of knowledge is so . . . so unpredictable, Bart.

BART: Well, everybody knows that.

SKYE: Could I say something? I'm really upset—

(*Skye is interrupted by Winston's entrance with a bowl of dog on a tray with spoons and napkins. Winston is singing a fanfare*)

WINSTON: Compliments of President Ferdinand Marcos and the First Lady!

EUGENE: What a smell!

JOCKO: Woof-woof-woof-woof-woof!

(*Winston sets down the tray and the men help themselves to dog*)

BART: Hand me a beer, would you, Eugene?

JOCKO: Winston, I'm going to see that you get an Oscar for this.

BART: Mmmmmmm-*mmmmmmmh!* Ahhh! Brrrr! Yummy yummy! Deee-lish! Winston, my boy, you are a *good boy!* This is dog!

JOCKO: There is only one thing that could make me happier. If this was Benjie.

EUGENE: It's like beef but a little sweeter. You should really try it, Skye.

SKYE: I said *no!*

JOCKO: Yessir, this is—hey, just a minute, there's a . . . dog tag in here . . .

SKYE: What?

JOCKO: . . . Mr. Poochie . . .

SKYE: That's not funny, Jocko!

(*The others laugh. They make exaggerated dog noises*)

BART: Yumyumyumyumyumyumyumyumyumyumyum—

JOCKO: Goodgoodgoodgoodgoodgoodgoodgoodgoodgoodgoodgoodgoodgood—

EUGENE: Mmmmmmmmmwowwowowowowowowowowowwowmmmmmmmmmmyumyumyumyumyumyumyumy—

JOCKO: Why don't you take off your gun and join us, Winston?

WINSTON: Oh, no . . . I cannot do that, Jocko.

JOCKO: What do these Muslims have, a frogman unit? The chances of us being assassinated or thrown into the trunk of a foreign car while the typhoon's going on are pretty slim.

WINSTON: You know how Muslim kill you? Cut off head, cut open stomach, put head inside stomach.

JOCKO: Muslims have always had a high capacity for whimsy. Where does one go to become a bodyguard, Winston? Pass me a beer, would you, Bart?

WINSTON: I spend . . . six months at Subic Bay. Shoot, fight, psychology. I can shoot the beak off a parrot at twenty meters.

JOCKO: How many bodyguards does Milo McGee McGarr have?

WINSTON: Six. Three all day. Three all night.

JOCKO: Six bodyguards for one person, one bodyguard for the four of us. Well, he is the resident genius, I guess.

WINSTON: I . . . am not your bodyguard, Jocko. I . . . am only Eugene's bodyguard.

JOCKO: (*Surprised*) Oh yeah?

EUGENE: Why don't you take some stew downstairs, Winston?

WINSTON: Thank you, Eugene. (*He exits with a bowl of dog*)

SKYE: Could I say something? I really feel no one's actually relating what's on their mind, you know? I mean all these limericks and put-downs, these dog jokes, all these things are just headtrips, just intellectualizing. You see what I'm saying?

JOCKO: Sure, we'll talk about you, if you want.

SKYE: That's not what I meant, Jocko! Oh, see, you're all so defended, so blocking up what you feel!

EUGENE: I feel like baying at the moon.

JOCKO: Go ahead.

(*Eugene howls*)

BART: *American Werewolf.* I coulda' done that.

SKYE: I really feel good about myself, you know?

JOCKO: Yeah, me too.

SKYE: No, like really. I mean like I make a living. I have dimensional, nonsuffocating relationships. Hobbies.

JOCKO: Now, there's a nice grown-up word, isn't it? Hobbies. Tell us about your hobbies.

SKYE: Oh, well, my main one is photography. I love photography.

JOCKO: Christ—just what the world needs—more photographs.

BART: The ruination of the twentieth century is the pocket instamatic.

JOCKO: The mania the world has for pictures—television, movies, photographs. So lazy. Pictures do all the work for you. Whatever happened to verbs?

SKYE: Boy, you people are real skunks, you know that? You set me up, and I give you a sincere, honest answer, and you just dump all over me! God, you're all so held in, so emotionally corseted! This is like living in ancient England with a bunch of Victorians. Got your girdle on, Jocko?

EUGENE: Christ, you two ought to get married.

SKYE: Now that's a real smartass remark.

JOCKO: You know what your problem is, Skye honey? Your life is like your limerick. You think you can write a limerick and live your life by just spilling your guts on the table. But a limerick has rules, standards, even a history—it's not supposed to be an anarchistic expression of random emotions, and neither is your life!

SKYE: Oh, well, what do you all talk about that's so substantial? Dog jokes and whether this movie's gonna get finished or not! Well, who cares if this movie gets finished or not? Who cares about some stupid little war in Angola, Africa? If it doesn't get finished, so what,

you move on to something else. Build something else,
Eugene!

EUGENE: Build something else?

BART: Hey, some of us aren't doing a naked thirty-second
walk-on and then flying to Tokyo for a cosmetics com-
mercial, buddy!

EUGENE: I've been working on this picture for three goddam years! See all this? I built two whole African villages, a thirty-meter lagoon, tank depots . . .

SKYE: Three years?

EUGENE: Thirty-six locations! Two thousand costumes!
You dumb bitch!!

JOCKO: Easy, Eugene. Let's see your Wattage Therapy
get you out of this.

SKYE: Shut up, Jocko. You don't know the first thing
about Wattage Therapy! Well, I'll tell you something,
Jocko. You are a loser, and you're about to become a
big loser the split second this rainwater's over. And you
want to know why?

JOCKO: Not really.

SKYE: You know, 'cause you and Milo are such good
friends, that he and I have been sleeping together.
That's one of the ways I got this part . . .

JOCKO: No—I didn't know that!

SKYE: You didn't? Well, maybe I shouldn't've let that slip. But based on that, I can tell you officially from the mouth of the horse that because of your inability to come up with an ending he liked, Milo's bringing in Dave Hawk from the coast right after the typhoon and sending you back.

JOCKO: Yeah? (*After a pause*) Fortunately, I've got an ending.

SKYE: Oh, he knows you'll come up with an ending. An ending he'd *like*, I said. Now I am going outside to take a shower. (*She picks up the kerosene lamp and exits into her room*)

JOCKO: Dave Hawk. Is that true?

(*Skye does not answer and is gone*)

JOCKO: Oh, Christ, I knew it, I knew it . . . Dave Hawk.

(*Jocko exits into his room. Bart crosses up and sits, looking out the window. Eugene crosses to Skye's room and knocks on her door*)

EUGENE: Look, Skye, I'm sorry. I didn't mean to blow up. I'm just so worried about the picture. It's . . . I feel so . . . uh . . . frustrated . . .

SKYE: (*Entering*) The girl always gets to be the victim in a thing like this, you know? Everybody's hostility finds a focus. But this is ridiculous! I'm famous for getting along with people!

EUGENE: Oh, you're getting along fine . . .

SKYE: I know all everybody wants to do is lay me, but what'm I supposed to do? If I make it with one of you, the other two'll just get pissed off, and then it's all over.

EUGENE: Is that the only reason we haven't made it? 'Cause you think it'll piss off them?

SKYE: Of course. This is very political.

EUGENE: But they won't mind!

SKYE: Oh, yes, they will. He will . . . Jocko.

EUGENE: I'll talk to them, they won't mind. I know it! Hey, and here I've been worried that I was doing something wrong—

SKYE: He's just psycho! God, all that hostility stuff about L.A.—I mean I love L.A. and everything it stands for! How can you be such good friends with him?

EUGENE: Oh, we're not such good friends.

SKYE: Did you really faint at your own wedding?

EUGENE: Yeah.

SKYE: How come?

EUGENE: There was a lot of pressure.

SKYE: But hey, I would've thought like you'd be great under pressure.

EUGENE: Not with her.

SKYE: She really gave you those scars?

EUGENE: Yeah.

SKYE: Wow.

EUGENE: But look, I don't want to talk about her. I want to talk about you.

SKYE: Man, I'm never gonna let this happen again. Hold me a second, would you, Eugene? (*They embrace*) You're much more creative than Jocko.

EUGENE: Listen, Skye, they can't stay up all night. When they go to bed . . .

SKYE: Oh, I don't know, Eugene.

EUGENE: They won't mind, I'm telling you. Later, okay?

SKYE: It's real complicated, Eugene . . .

EUGENE: No, it's not. Later! Okay? Look, I really like you, Skye.

SKYE: (*Absently*) Oh, and I really like you, too, Eugene. I have to change for my shower.

EUGENE: Let me help you.

(*Eugene brings his hands under her blouse. Skye deftly stops him*)

SKYE: I'll do the rest.

(*Skye exits into her room, Eugene exits into his room, Jocko enters*)

JOCKO: My God, Dave Hawk. My whole life's been like this.

BART: Maybe you're in the wrong profession, lad.

JOCKO: No, Bart, I love the movies.

BART: But you're miserable, don't you see that?

JOCKO: I grew up on the movies, Bart.

BART: Oh, I know boys like you; spend all day in movie theaters. To you the movies are real life. I didn't see my first picture till I was twenty-four. I knew right away it was just tricks. Did my first job in '56 at Warners: a car-wreck skull bash; good work. Gave me perspective. Making movies is a skill, Jocko! You shouldn't be fooled by it. I didn't get my values from the movies. Nobody worth anything does. Ever hear of a king or a pope or an artist who was seriously influenced by the movies? Think Picasso went to the movies a lot? Movies are things you outgrow, boy. Look at the people who go to them: kids. The only people whose lives revolve around the movies are *A*, people in the movie business; and *B*, people like you who don't know which end is up. You're in the wrong profession, lad.

JOCKO: No, I'm not.

BART: Maybe you're in the right profession but the wrong area. Maybe you should be a writer but not of screenplays and not of novels. Maybe you should take up poetry and become really irrelevant. Maybe you're in the right profession and the right area but doomed to eternal second-rateness. You might even kill yourself, I see that now. No wife, no children . . . you're really all alone, aren't you? A very sad figure when you think about it. It wouldn't be so inconsiderate.

JOCKO: I promise you one thing. I won't kill myself before I kill you.

BART: Big talker, big talker—you were always a big talker, Jocko.

JOCKO: Whadda ya mean "always"? You've only known me three weeks. Besides, I've got another ending for *Parabola of Death*.

BART: Yeah? What is it?

JOCKO: I don't want to discuss it with the make-up man.

BART: Oh-ho.

JOCKO: God, Dave Hawk—I knew it.

(*Skye enters dressed in a bikini and carrying a towel,
     shampoo, and brush*)

SKYE: I'm going outside to take my shower.

(*Skye leaves her towel and exits*)

BART: You know what I hate? All the Irishness on this
    picture. Milo's Irish, the crew's all Irish, the characters
    names are Irish, even I'm Irish. (*Adopting an Irish ac-
    cent*) Oh mither, kin ya din, oh mither, Mither Macree,
    may the road rise to meet ye, may the wind always be
    at your back. Shelaleigh, Shelaleigh. The little darlin'.
    And bairn, bairn, they're always sayin', "I want to have
    your bairn, Johnny."

JOCKO: That's Scottish, Bart.

BART: Bairn? No, it isn't—they say it all the time. And
    they're always saying things with "oi" in them, you
    know? Oi, oi, oi, oi!

JOCKO: I think that's the Jews, Bart.

BART: No, no, not oi, oi, bigmouth—oi, oi, like Oirish,
    Oirish.

JOCKO: Oh.

BART: Jesus Christ—the Jews? You think I'd make a mis-
    take like that? In this business? Come on!

(*Eugene enters wearing a colorful Hawaiian shirt. He crosses to Skye's room and looks in*)

JOCKO: Hey, snazzy shirt. (*He crosses to the upstage window and opens the screen*)

EUGENE: Where's whatshername?

JOCKO: (*Pointing outside*) Taking her shower.

(*Eugene and Jocko stare out the window*)

BART: (*Oblivious to what they are doing*) You know Milo had three hundred cases of Guinness stout shipped over here special?

JOCKO: God, she's astonishing, isn't she . . .

BART: I mean, what's the matter with San Miguel? Beer's the one thing they do right in the Philippines. Beer and dog. I mean if Milo's so bloody Irish, how come he isn't a cop or the head of some union?

JOCKO: Milo hates unions.

BART: Milo McGee McGarr hates unions? How can you not like unions and still be Irish? And what's so Irish about him anyway? He doesn't sound Irish, he doesn't look Irish; he doesn't even smoke a pipe. (*He turns and sees them looking out the window*) What are you guys looking at? (*He joins them at the window*)

JOCKO: What about your fingernails . . .

(They all stand staring for quite a while, then quickly, they break and all resume casual positions around the room. Skye enters soaking wet and looking fabulous. Eugene picks up the towel and starts to dry her off)

EUGENE: Cold?

SKYE: No. Just a minute, Eugene. I've got something to say, Jocko.

JOCKO: Hey, I don't want to argue . . .

SKYE: This isn't an argument. You know what I said about you getting fired? It isn't true. I mean I never had that conversation with Milo.

BART: It wasn't true? What was it—a joke?

SKYE: No, it wasn't a joke—it was Wattage Therapy, Phase Two.

BART: By God, you got him! You got this little monkey Jocko boy, didn't you?

SKYE: That's how we're taught to defend ourselves against emotion-whittlers like you.

BART: What do you think of her now?

JOCKO: *(After a pause, reading)*
    A man who lived in twin towers
    Liked to make love to his flowers.

"The only problem," said he,
"Are the thorns when I pee,
Which I pluck out without luck for hours."

BART: Don't give me that! She got you, she got you, got you good!

JOCKO: Shut up, Bart. The girl's a moron!

SKYE: God, doesn't anything get through to you!

BART: I will not shut up! Are you trying to bully me again, Jocko? Set me up because by some fluke of nature I happen to look like a former Nobel Prize winner? Well, it won't work!

JOCKO: Oh, Christ!

EUGENE: Which Nobel Prize winner?

BART: (*Amazed*) Hemingway!

EUGENE: *Ernest* Hemingway?

BART: Of course, Ernest Hemingway!

SKYE: I've had it with you, Jocko! You little squirt!

EUGENE: But you don't look anything like Ernest Hemingway. Except for the beard, maybe!

BART: What?!

SKYE: Just because you get depressed more doesn't mean you're smarter, you know.

EUGENE: Your knees are too fat, your nose is flatter than his, and he'd never wear his clothes in that defeated way you do.

BART: Well, those are very small things, Eugene, very small things. Why, I'm known as "Papa" from one end of the peninsula to the other! Come on—"Paris was fine that year, and the making love was fine. And the writing was good, and it was fine." Hey, come on!

EUGENE: I didn't say you don't know your stuff. You just don't look like him.

SKYE: Now, I really see through you—Dr. Sonny was right! You're just hassling me because Phase Two worked.

JOCKO: You have to be lobotomized to believe that stupid doctor. That's just insults. Where'd he get his degree? Don Rickles University?

BART: "And he took the fish, and it was a fine fish, and he saw the eyes of DiMaggio, the eyes of the great DiMaggio."

EUGENE: Who cares, Bart?

JOCKO: Insults and telling lies to hurt people—that's new?

BART: "And Scott was a good writer, maybe a great writer, but a wasted one, who piddled away his talent and had the smallest capacity for drink I'd ever known." (*Bart is nearly hysterical. In a voice that shakes the rafters*) NOT LOOK LIKE ERNEST HEMINGWAAAAAY!!!!

EUGENE: You wanna arm-wrestle? Come on, Papa, let's go!

(*They instantly lock arms. Eugene pins Bart at will and grabs his left hand*)

EUGENE: Come on, come on, left hand, left hand!

(*Eugene pins Bart again; Bart falls to the floor. He is furious*)

BART: (*Stands up*) NOT LOOK LIKE ERNEST HEMINGWAY? I *AM* ERNEST HEMINGWAY!

(*Bart stomps into his room and slams the door, but the door takes a beat and pops open. Bart reappears*)

BART: (*Quietly*) Would you put the chair up please, Jocko?

(*Bart exits into his room. Jocko puts a chair up against the door. Skye has come to some kind of conclusion*)

SKYE: Would you excuse us for a minute, Eugene?

EUGENE: What?

SKYE: I'd like to talk to Jocko alone.

EUGENE: Why?

SKYE: I want to.

EUGENE: Knock on my door when you're through.

SKYE: I don't think so, Eugene. Good night.

EUGENE: Skye . . .

SKYE: Good night, Eugene.

(*Eugene's fury is buried in a ball somewhere in his small intestine. His fists are clenched so tight that his knuckles are bloodless. He exits into his room and quietly closes the door. Skye takes off her robe*)

SKYE: You win. Let's go.

JOCKO: What? Where?

SKYE: To bed.

JOCKO: What?

SKYE: I can't stand to be ridiculed. You really made me believe you hated me.

JOCKO: I did, huh?

SKYE: At first I thought it was a new approach, and real obvious—remember when you told me off about being a stew and a Playmate? My take was—hey, is he coming on to me! But now after these four days or whatever it is, you're not kidding. You may really hate me.

JOCKO: More than life itself.

SKYE: I don't believe you, but it's very seductive. Let's go.

JOCKO: No.

SKYE: No? Why not?

JOCKO: I don't want to.

SKYE: My God, you like little boys, don't you?

JOCKO: That's it, that's it; whenever you don't want to go to bed with a woman, suddenly you're homosexual.

SKYE: Then how come you won't go to bed with me?

JOCKO: Going to bed with you is not the only alternative to homosexuality.

SKYE: I am prime meat! Do you know how many men out there would kill for a piece of this pie? Guys hump their pillows thinking of me!

JOCKO: You see the whole world in terms of a pass, don't you?

SKYE: What?

JOCKO: Somebody likes you, you think it's a pass; somebody hates you, you think *that's* a pass. You're way beyond being a sex object—you're a sex subject. Your life is defined by sex—and not by its pleasure, but by its power. Right this minute, you don't care about me; you just want to make peace in case we're stuck here for three months. Yes, you are prime meat, but no I'm not homosexual and no I'm not going to bed with you.

SKYE: Well, why did you come on to me like that? All night, all yesterday, the day before—

JOCKO: Who said I was coming on to you?

SKYE: Oh, don't kid me bub—I know a *tour de force* when I see one. All that putting me down, all that passion. Flattery by rejection. Where do you think I've been? You *do* want me, don't you? Don't you?

JOCKO: Maybe.

SKYE: Then why won't you go to bed with me?

JOCKO: You're . . . sick.

SKYE: What?

JOCKO: You're sick. You've got diarrhea, your breath is bad, your skin's clammy.

SKYE: I don't believe it.

JOCKO: I'm sorry, but the lifelong fantasy of a one-night stand with a Playmate of the Year doesn't include her having amoebic dysentery. Oh, but hey—what's your phone number? Y'know, in case we ever get back to L.A.

SKYE: 213-555-7986.

(*Jocko writes it down*)

JOCKO: And your address?

SKYE: 8979¼ Wonderland Avenue, Hollywood, California, 90048.

JOCKO: There really is a Wonderland Avenue?

SKYE: It's in the hills. Jocko, do I really look that bad?

JOCKO: No, no, you're very attractive, really. You're just . . . so . . . sick . . .

SKYE: Don't say it again, okay?

(*Jocko drinks an enormous amount from a bottle of vodka*)

SKYE: Hey, take it easy.

JOCKO: Just a little nightcap. Good night and so forth.

(*Jocko turns and stumbles over a chair. He recovers and slowly exits into his room. Skye then slowly crosses to*

each of the candle trays and blows out the candles.
After she has put out the third tray, Eugene enters,
unheard by Skye and slowly tai-chi's his way to the
center table just as Skye arrives there for the last tray
of candles. Eugene jumps onto the table just as she is
reaching for the tray)

EUGENE: Hi.

(Eugene holds her hand that holds the tray and blows
out the last candles. He puts the tray down and pulls
her to him. Skye resists him)

SKYE: What are you . . . ?

EUGENE: Oh, come on.

SKYE: No-o-o!

(Skye crosses to her room. Eugene cuts her off and takes
her hand. They slowly cross right, Eugene not letting
go of her)

EUGENE: What a day, huh?

SKYE: What do you mean?

(Skye gently spins out of Eugene's grasp and crosses
down right. Eugene follows)

EUGENE: I'll never forget this day. Do you like Ping-Pong?

SKYE: Eugene!

EUGENE: Come on! Do you like Ping-Pong?

(*Eugene begins to gently shadow-box with Skye*)

SKYE: Now and then, but as a participant, not as an observer.

(*Skye tries to cross to her room but Eugene grabs her wrist*)

SKYE: Oowww!

EUGENE: (*Holding her wrist*) Could you be more specific? About the Ping-Pong, I mean.

SKYE: I like to play the game but not to watch it all that much.

(*Skye breaks away and crosses to her room. Eugene crosses up and cuts her off again*)

EUGENE: Get me a cup of coffee.

SKYE: There isn't any coffee.

EUGENE: What!

SKYE: There's no hot water—you know that!

EUGENE: Run next door and get some!

SKYE: No-o-o!

EUGENE: What?

SKYE: NO!

(*Skye takes a step toward her room, and Eugene suddenly kicks her door closed. It swings open, but Skye has backed up, terrified*)

EUGENE: Sshhh! Everybody's sleeping.

(*Skye stands still for a second and then takes a step toward her room again. Eugene stops her with a "unh-unh," and he points to his room, indicating that there is where he wants her to go. Skye slowly backs right and starts crossing up to what Eugene thinks is his room. But on the way, Skye reaches Jocko's door and starts to scream for help, but Eugene quickly covers her mouth and pulls her away from Jocko's door and slowly closes it himself. He turns her around and suddenly punches her full across the mouth. She stumbles Downstage, and he follows, quickly grabbing her around the waist and behind the neck. Crossing left, he takes her and throws her into her own door. She screams in pain, but he is quickly on her, punching her in the stomach and face, mauling her against her door. One last punch sends her sprawling down on the floor. Eugene dances back, the victor of the battle. Winston comes running in with his gun drawn and points it at Eugene*)

WINSTON: Eugene!

EUGENE: Hey, Winston, boy, there's a famous American saying, "You can run, but you can't hide." It was a snap —a one-two combo to the kidneys, a left hook to the jaw, and she was in that place where alligators play trombones. *This* has been the thriller in Manila!

(*Eugene dances into his room and closes the door. Winston, totally confused, does not know what to do. He fires two shots into the shelf, Stage Right. Cans and supplies fall to the floor and the shelf collapses. Petrified, Winston runs out. After a beat, Bart enters from his room, quite drunk and carrying a flashlight. He has shaved off his beard. He does not see Skye lying unconscious on the floor, down left*)

BART: Hey, fellas—I'm all better now! I know I'm not Ernest Hemingway, are you kidding? See? All shaved off! Now, I don't even look like him! (*He opens the shutter and looks out the window*) Hey, it's stopped. The rain's stopped!

CURTAIN

ACT THREE

ACT THREE

The following morning.

Harsh and unpleasant daylight glares through the windows. The air is humid. Chickens, dogs, and pigs make incredible noise outside. The debris from the gunshots is swept up in a pile. On the center table sits a pot of coffee with cups around it. The electric light bulb is on again; the electricity is on. There are more empty bottles scattered around the stage, pieces of clothing, and a general mess. Jocko is typing on his typewriter at the center table. He rips out a sheet and throws it in the general direction of the wastebasket. He puts in another, types, and throws this one out, too. Again, he puts in another sheet, but this time he tears it out before typing a word. He rises and crosses to Skye's room. He knocks.

JOCKO: Skye? (*No answer. He knocks again*) Skye?

SKYE: Who is it?

JOCKO: Just me again.

SKYE: Where's Eugene?

JOCKO: Checking out the set. Don't worry. And Bart's not up yet. Would you like some coffee? It's not Nescafe . . .

SKYE: No. Oh, yes.

JOCKO: Milo's on his way. He should've been here half an hour ago. Milo can fix anything. (*To himself*) Except maybe helicopters that won't fly into frame.

(*Jocko pours a cup of coffee. Skye enters and we see her beaten face that is covered with bruises and cuts. He gives her the cup. She falls into his arms*)

SKYE: What am I going to do, Jocko? What am I going to do?

JOCKO: (*Nervously*) It's okay. It's okay. Milo'll fix everything, Skye, don't worry.

SKYE: I don't mean about this. I mean like is this how everybody reacts to me? You're a man.

JOCKO: No! Of course not! This hasn't happened before, has it?

SKYE: No, but they feel like it—I know it. I mean you were ready to kill me, Bart was ready to kill me, and that son of a bitch Eugene practically *did* kill me. Is that what people really think of me?

JOCKO: No! Skye—this wasn't your fault. It was his.

SKYE: But I make people mad, don't I? Always have—men and women. I've got to get some control over things. You know, like you.

JOCKO: Like me?

SKYE: Well, I mean at least you know what you're doing. I—

JOCKO: Skye, I haven't a clue what I'm doing. Last night Bart rattled off fifteen professions I should be doing instead of writing this screenplay. And you know something? They all sounded great.

SKYE: Well, why don't you do one of them?

JOCKO: I don't know, Skye, I—

SKYE: Listen, Jocko. I don't have time to talk you into anything right now. I've got to be real selfish here, okay?

JOCKO: Sure, I don't blame you.

(*Skye starts to exit into her room*)

SKYE: Oh, thank you for taking care of me.

JOCKO: You're welcome.

SKYE: It was real nice of you. (*She exits into her room*)

JOCKO: Milo'll be here in a minute. (*He crosses to his typewriter*) Well, do something.

(*Jocko exits into his room. Bart enters, hungover, and sees the fallen shelf*)

BART: What's this supposed to be? (*He crosses to the center table and pours a cup of coffee. Then he hears the neighborhood chickens outside*) Shut up out there, shut up! You chickens! Shut up! Goddam chickens never learn. Winston! Winston! God, it's hot!

(*Winston enters from outside*)

WINSTON: Yes, Bart?

BART: Got anything for breakfast?

WINSTON: Uh, everything, Bart! Bacon . . . toast . . . mango . . . papaya . . . egg . . .

BART: Give me four of everything—six bacon, two toast, a mango, half a papaya, and three eggs—but make sure they're cooked!

WINSTON: Okay, Bart.

BART: I want those eggs poached *and* fried, boiled *and* baked. I want 'em burned black so nothing can grow on 'em, heh, heh.

(*Winston has noticed that Bart's beard is gone and starts to laugh*)

BART: Why, what's the matter, little fella?

WINSTON: (*Thinking quickly*) Oh . . . nothing, Bart. I shouldn't . . . shoot the shelf.

BART: You did this? You gotta learn a little control, son. Aww, don't worry about it—we can clean this up in no time. Get me breakfast, all right, lad?

(*Winston exits*)

BART: I thought you only shot the beaks off parrots.

(*Bart sits at the center table with his coffee. Skye enters. At first Bart doesn't notice her, but when he sees her he is aghast*)

BART: My God, what happened?

SKYE: I don't want to talk about it.

BART: My God, my God. It's beautiful. (*He is torn between personal horror and professional fascination. He snatches up his Polaroid and pops off a few shots*)

SKYE: Bart! Bart, please.

BART: The colors—it's like the inside of the body during surgery!

SKYE: Bart!

BART: Beautiful! I won't show these to a soul, honest. Who did this to you?

SKYE: Eugene.

BART: But I thought he liked you . . .

SKYE: Guess not. Milo's on his way here.

BART: Milo's coming here?

SKYE: What's the matter?

BART: I don't want him to see me like this. (*He exits into his room*)

SKYE: You don't . . . ? Hey, what happened to your beard?

(*The sound of a helicopter approaches and gets louder, so loud it appears the thing is going to land in the living room. Skye, frightened, runs into her room*)

SKYE: My clothes!

(*Skye exits into her room. Jocko enters*)

JOCKO: Oh, Christ!

(*Jocko exits into his room. Skye enters and runs out up left. Jocko enters again with a pile of typing paper, inserts a sheet in the typewriter, and begins to type furiously. After a few beats, he crosses up to the window, then returns to his chair, picking up the wastebasket and tossing papers around him. He then resumes typing. Milo enters)*

JOCKO: (*Feigning surprise*) Milo!

MILO: Now that's what I like to see! Whatta we got? (*He tears out paper from typewriter*) Qwertyuiop and ½. Asdfghjkl; apostrophe. Nice work, Jocko. You know what I did? I solved the helicopter problem, Jocko.

JOCKO: You did? How?

MILO: I finally figured out the reason those helicopter pilots weren't flying into frame wasn't on account of the pilots—it was 'cause the Filipino general in charge was waiting for his bribe. So, five minutes ago I gave it to him: twenty-five grand! They'll fly into frame now. Where's the girl?

JOCKO: In there. Twenty-five grand. You don't fool around, do you?

MILO: Gets the day off to a good start. Better for you than coffee and a much bigger rush. Christ, this place looks like that little girl's room in *The Exorcist*. What happened here?

JOCKO: You really want to know?

MILO: Look, Jocko, I been trapped in Manila for four days like a stuck pig, I got a million bucks of equipment out there sinking into the mud, the Seligstein

boys are flying in this afternoon to tell me if I'm al-
lowed to finish my picture, and two hours ago I get a
radio call that my production designer just beat up my
Playmate and could go to jail for the rest of his life. So
I haven't got time for you to be witty and arch and all
that crap. Noël Coward is dead. Just tell me what happened.

JOCKO: Last night, after the rest of us passed out—about
two a.m.—Eugene attacked Skye. Beat her up.

MILO: I was afraid of that. Eugene's done this before, you
know.

JOCKO: What?

MILO: Once, when we were making *Quicksilver* in Texas,
he got involved with this beautiful teenager; at the end
of shooting, he broke her jaw. Then during *Control of
the Skies*, in L.A., he beat up a black girl he was supposed to be in love with. We had to pay that girl in
Texas a bundle.

JOCKO: Wait a minute—you knew he'd done this before
and you let him stay here with her?

MILO: Hey, I practically killed myself trying to get him
outta here with that helicopter four days ago, remember?

JOCKO: Why didn't you warn somebody?

MILO: Oh, what, were you gonna stop him, Jocko? Good luck.

JOCKO: It's amazing. I was the one always giving her a hard time. Not him.

MILO: Oh, what, more crap about L.A.? Jesus, Jocko, you really think that's a serious philosophical issue, don't you? Well, it isn't. You just don't like L.A. 'cause you've never had any success there. I know you, Jocko, if the Seligstein boys would produce a screenplay of yours, you'd be playing tennis and driving a Mercedes tomorrow. It's a fake issue, that New York versus L.A. crap. It's covering up for something else and you should face it.

JOCKO: Look, what are you gonna do about her?

MILO: I want to finish this picture, Jocko, and I want to finish it with Eugene. He's the only one who can rebuild these sets. If the Seligstein boys hear he's going to be thrown in jail, they'll pull the plug on me without getting off the plane. That's how good he is. And besides, Eugene's a friend of mine. We've been to Paris together, we go to dinner all the time, we're friends. Goddammit, this pisses me off!

JOCKO: Did he beat up his wife?

MILO: I don't know. We never talk about this, you know. All we ever talk about is how to get out of it.

JOCKO: Well, maybe she'll accept a payoff if that's what you want.

MILO: I don't *like* paying off people, Jocko. I don't *like* bribing generals. I'm supposed to be the exception, remember. The honest one. And what if she doesn't accept a payoff? What if she presses charges? They'll put Eugene in jail for ten years—plus the year he'll just be waiting around for the trial. You ever been in one of these Filipino jails, Jocko? They're like the ones in India and Vietnam—cowshit for a floor, diseased rapists coming at you, guards beating you with batons, all that. This is one of those places.

JOCKO: What're you gonna do?

MILO: Well, we have two choices. Talk her out of pressing charges. Or kill her. (*After a pause*) Just kidding, Jocko. Look, ask her to come out, would you?

(*Jocko knocks and enters her room. He comes right out*)

JOCKO: She's not there. Winston! Winston!

MILO: What?

(*Winston runs in*)

JOCKO: Winston, have you seen Skye?

WINSTON: She went to bury her clothes in the mud.

MILO: Christ. Winston, will you go there and bring her here?

WINSTON: Oh, yes sir. (*He exits*)

MILO: Bury her clothes in the mud. God, I hate this picture. I tell ya, the next movie I make is gonna be in Paris. It's gonna star Audrey Hepburn and Cary Grant —if I can coax him out of retirement. A nice little romantic thriller with clever dialogue. All white interiors, all shot on sound stages with maybe a nice chase sequence up the Sacre Coeur. No tropical plants, no fawning natives, and no helicopters: mainly no goddam helicopters.

JOCKO: Who'll you substitute for Cary Grant if you can't coax him out of retirement?

MILO: There is no substitute for Cary Grant. Hey, is she coming? My other pictures weren't like this, you know. The budgets on all my other pictures combined won't equal this one; somehow it just got away from me. I don't know how. But I'm gonna finish it.

JOCKO: You really think so?

MILO: I know it, Jocko. There are only two things in this world I cannot do: I cannot comprehend the needless suffering of millions of starving children all over this planet, and I cannot direct comedies. Also, I have a little pretentious streak in me I have to watch out for. But lick a few helicopters and a little bad weather?

Natural disasters and uncooperative machinery are my forte. Where is the girl? You know what I'd really like to do? Make one huge blockbuster like Georgie Lucas or Francis or Spielberg, take home forty, fifty million bucks, and quit all this. This isn't exciting, directing a movie.

JOCKO: Careful—twelve thousand college kids are going to switch majors if they hear you say that. And I thought you made a bundle on *Control of the Skies.*

MILO: Everybody did. They thought I made thirty million. No way. I made eight, but I didn't make thirty. No, this isn't exciting. I mean whatta we do here—two shots a day, one at sunset, one at sunrise. The rest of the time's spent throwing footballs around and eating coconuts. The only excitement out here's when a typhoon comes along or somebody gets bit by a snake. It's all logistics, directing—all I worry about is moving cameras from shot to shot, getting those helicopters up in the air, and whether the crew's gonna get pissed off about lunch again. The one thing I don't have time for is the content of the movie.

JOCKO: Yeah, I've seen you work; all you do is get stoned with the actors and give them permission to change my lines.

MILO: I like you, Jocko. You're just bright enough that when I beat you in an argument, I feel a genuine sense of accomplishment. Y'know the only exciting thing about making a movie anymore? The deal. That's the real drama—sittin' in the office at Paramount thinking up outrageous demands: "Ten points, final cut, my own helicopter, and thirty cases of Guinness shipped to the Philippines." The more outrageous your demands, the more they want you. I mean, who likes Guinness? Those execs don't know if they're getting another *Godfather* or just a *Honky Tonk Freeway*. I'll tell you what's exciting, Jocko. Making money. I don't mean having money or spending money, I mean making it. You probably think making money's immoral, because you're a boring thirties socialist and you've never made any—

JOCKO: How can I be a boring thirties socialist? I was born in 1948.

MILO: Boring thirties socialism is a state of mind, Jocko. The great American adventure isn't being a rock star or a pro basketball player. It's business. There is nothing as creative or as romantic as business in America. I got sixteen subsidiary companies have nothing to do with the picture business, from a newspaper in Okmulgee, Oklahoma, to a seed company in Sauk City, Wisconsin. And every one of them is more exciting than directing a movie. I dreamed them up, I put them together, and I make them work. Best of all, not one of them is unionized. I have to pay them more and treat them better, but at least they work hard in return and I get to say who's fired. No bunch of goons is going to do to me what they've done to the picture business. I am thirty-two years old and having the time of my life. And that pisses a lot of people off, which is almost as much fun as making money.

(*Skye enters. Milo is aghast at her face. He is about to move to her when Eugene enters with mud halfway up his pants*)

MILO: Jesus!

(*Skye sees Eugene, screams, and starts throwing things at him. Jocko tries to stop her*)

MILO: Get downstairs! Get out of here! Get out! Grab her, Jocko! Grab her! Don't just stand there!

(*Eugene runs out. Jocko calms her down*)

MILO: (*To Eugene*) What's that on your legs?

EUGENE: (*Offstage*) Mud!

MILO: Is it that deep?

EUGENE: (*Offstage*) The generator truck's stuck in more than a foot of mud!

MILO: Oh, Christ, the generator . . .

SKYE: (*Furiously*) You want to pay attention to me or you want to pay attention to your goddam movie!! (*She slams her room door on her exit*)

MILO: (*To Eugene*) Stay down there till I tell you! (*He crosses to Skye's door and knocks*) Skye? Skye, you're right. Eugene's downstairs. I'm sorry, I just have to find out what trouble we're in. But hey—I really do want to talk to you. Come on, it's very important.

(*Skye slowly comes out of her room*)

MILO: How are you?

SKYE: I want to go home.

MILO: Of course. The *Jet Ranger*'s right outside. We can get you on a plane for L.A. this afternoon.

SKYE: I mean I can't be in the picture this way, can I?

MILO: No.

SKYE: I'm going to put him in a Filipino slammer for twenty years.

MILO: It's all right now.

SKYE: Look at this, Milo! I won't be able to work for months! And who knows what I'll look like then? I may never be able to work again!

MILO: Sure you will . . .

(*Skye cries suddenly. Milo holds her*)

MILO: It's all right now. We're all right with you. Come on, sit down for a moment, Skye. Breathe in . . . that's it.

SKYE: God, my looks used to be in the top one percentile of the nation. I used to be compared to great beauties!

MILO: What can I do to help you now, Skye?

SKYE: I don't know—I'm real confused. Maybe I can do something else on this picture.

MILO: Well, you're obviously a bright and intelligent girl. I think we could make very good use of you behind the scenes on this picture. If you'd be interested in staying on.

SKYE: I don't know.

MILO: How about this: how about doing some editing with David Dokken? Cut my last two pictures—two Oscars. It's a great way to learn the business.

JOCKO: Editing with Dokken? That normally takes years.

SKYE: Gee, editing'd be cool.

MILO: We'll assign you to the editing team directly under him. Except that you'd be in L.A., of course, and he's in Manila.

SKYE: Yeah, I'm not working in Manila. Or anywhere else in the South Pacific. Boy, did Rodgers and Hammerstein get this place wrong.

MILO: You could be on liaison assignment at home. After we cut the film in Manila, we send it back to L.A. for

Moe Seligstein to see. You could go to the rushes with Moe Seligstein every week.

JOCKO: Moe Seligstein! Nobody gets to do that.

MILO: We'd arrange it so you could just be in on all phases of the picture. No figurehead stuff—real work. See the rushes with Moe Seligstein, give your opinions about the picture, take meetings . . .

SKYE: Oh, come on, Milo, Moe Seligstein'd never listen to me!

JOCKO: Now see, Skye, what Milo's trying to say . . .

MILO: Quiet, Jocko. I'm not *trying* to say anything. I *am* saying it. I don't need an interpreter. Tell me, Skye, we've never had much of a chance to talk. Tell me about yourself. You have an old man?

SKYE: I sort of go with the doctor who founded Wattage Therapy.

MILO: Wattage Therapy! I've heard that gets fantastic results.

SKYE: You see, Jocko.

MILO: Jocko doesn't like Wattage Therapy?

SKYE: Oh, he says it's based on Don Rickles. Actually it is pretty stupid.

JOCKO: It is?

SKYE: Yeah—under tauntlets and insulting people. It's moronic, right, Jocko?

JOCKO: I'm amazed.

MILO: You're obviously an intelligent girl. Is this what you always want to be—an actress?

SKYE: Well, that and a photographer.

MILO: Photographer? Do you know Jackie Petalba?

SKYE: Jackie Petalba? Oh, wow!

MILO: What if I could get you on some shoots with Jackie Petalba?

SKYE: Wow! Oh, my God!

MILO: But you have to be really serious about this, Skye.

SKYE: Oh, I am—I'm really serious about photography.

MILO: Okay, then, pack; we'll fly to Manila in the *Jet Ranger*, and you'll be back home by tomorrow morning. Or why not spend a couple of days in Hawaii on the way? We'll pick up the tab.

SKYE: No, no, I have to get right back and see my doctor.

MILO: Oh yeah? Does Wattage Therapy help with this kind of thing?

SKYE: Oh, no, he wouldn't have a clue what to do with this. My real doctor. This is really neat of you, Milo. Photography lessons with Jackie Petalba . . .

MILO: Uh-huh.

SKYE: Liaison editing in L.A.

MILO: Oh, that, too?

SKYE: Yeah, and weekly screenings with Moe Selig-stein . . .

MILO: I thought you didn't care about that—

SKYE: I care.

MILO: Okay. Sure.

SKYE: A week of R and R in Hawaii . . .

MILO: I thought you wanted to go straight home to L.A.

SKYE: Oh, this is after I go straight home to L.A.

MILO: Oh. Sure.

SKYE: And your next picture?

MILO: Oh, well, I can't promise you anything on that. I don't even know what it is—but I guarantee you strong consideration.

SKYE: That's all I care about, Milo. I don't want to bust anybody's balls or anything. Besides, by then I'll be a much better actress. I'm going to take daily voice lessons and learn how to fence, and, you know, what the difference between Shakespeare and Congreve and Shaw is. See, Jocko?

JOCKO: That's great, Skye. Really great.

MILO: Sounds very exciting.

SKYE: You're not wrong about everything, Jocko, you know? (*To Milo*) Oh, and you are going to have to give me a big pile of money.

MILO: How much?

SKYE: One hundred thousand dollars.

MILO: One hundred thousand dollars? One hundred thousand dollars. Okay.

SKYE: One hundred thousand dollars in some way I won't be taxed.

MILO: How about cash? The day you arrive in L.A.

SKYE: Delivered in a leather attaché case—just like in the movies?

MILO: All right.

SKYE: One hundred thousand and those opportunities.

MILO: Right.

(*They shake hands*)

SKYE: Okay. Now I'll sign your release.

MILO: What release?

SKYE: Oh, come on, Milo. You're not going to give me any of these things without me signing a release.

(*Milo slowly pulls out the release form*)

MILO: Perhaps you'd like a job in my legal department?

JOCKO: I think there's something about you I didn't quite grasp . . .

(*Skye studies the release form*)

SKYE: I can't sign this.

MILO: Why not?

SKYE: You're asking me to give up my right to press charges against Eugene. I'll never do that.

MILO: Well, what do you think all these "opportunities" are for?

SKYE: That's so I won't sue you or Moe Seligstein or talk to the press. Doesn't have anything to do with whether I nail that son of a bitch Eugene or not.

MILO: Oh, why not let us take care of that, Skye . . . ?

SKYE: Let you take care of it! Look at this face! You think I'd give up my one crack at revenge for what you just offered me? Unh-unh!

JOCKO: Skye, as you know, Milo is a very powerful man. But in Hollywood, power can work in a negative as well as a positive way, and . . .

MILO: Jocko, you're brilliant, but you're a little heavy-handed. When I need a hatchet man, I'll call one.

JOCKO: Christ, is that what I've turned into in all this? Your hatchet man?

MILO: Skye, this is the . . .

JOCKO: Wait a minute, Milo—let her prosecute him!

MILO: What? Why?

JOCKO: Because that guy Eugene is a creep, goddammit! He's a megalomaniacal creep who thinks because he can build and blow up fake villages and tank depots for a movie he can do the same thing with people. (*Gesturing to Skye*) *This* is real life! You can't treat this like that!

MILO: Anything else?

JOCKO: Yes. Say something nice to her. She just got beat up by a psychotic power-mad control freak in the middle of the night. You know what it's like here at night? Very . . . fucking . . . dark!

MILO: That's very touching, Jocko, but when you're dealing with a hundred thousand dollars in an attaché case at the airport, things are a little beyond the say-something-nice stage.

JOCKO: Is that right? Is this beyond that?

(*Skye nods*)

JOCKO: Oh. I'm sorry, Milo. Sorry, Skye.

SKYE: That's all right, Jocko.

MILO: Skye, listen to me. You're a smart girl. I said that before and I didn't mean it, but I mean it now. I've got a problem. Eugene shouldn't have done that to you; but I categorically cannot finish this picture without him, and I intend to finish this picture. I don't know what you want—to become a movie star or a photographer or head of Paramount, but I think you could get whatever one of those you wanted. Now there must be something besides putting Eugene in jail that will satisfy your justifiable desire for revenge—and I'm willing to listen to any idea you've got.

(*Skye thinks for a moment*)

SKYE: Okay. I want to beat him up.

MILO: What?

SKYE: That's it—I want to beat him up.

JOCKO: My God.

MILO: Are you kidding?

SKYE: That's the only thing that's gonna make me feel better.

MILO: Beating him up's gonna make you feel better?

SKYE: Yup. Beating me up made him feel better.

MILO: (*After a moment*) Eugene! (*He exits*)

JOCKO: It's brilliant! It's so symmetrical.

SKYE: You think it's immoral?

JOCKO: An eye for an eye isn't exactly the cornerstone of our penal code.

SKYE: I don't care.

JOCKO: You believe in capital punishment?

SKYE: I do for him.

(*Eugene enters sheepishly as Skye clears away debris*)

MILO: (*Offstage*) Hey, Jocko, come on down a minute, will ya?

(*Jocko exits. Eugene moves closer to Skye. She makes sure the table is between them*)

EUGENE: I'd . . . really like to . . . apologize. I . . .

SKYE: I know you're sorry. What else?

EUGENE: I don't know why I did it . . . I . . . I . . . I'm not very articulate. I'm just . . . sorry. I . . . I . . . (*He stutters, unable to say anything else for a few seconds*)

SKYE: I want to beat the shit out of you, Eugene. For the same reason you beat the shit out of me.

EUGENE: Which is what?

SKYE: We're both getting back at somebody. Only I'm more direct. I'm getting back at you. I don't know who you're getting back at—your mother, your old lady, I don't know. And I don't care. All I know is this is gonna make me feel better.

EUGENE: For how long do you want to do this?

SKYE: Until I get tired of it.

(*There is another long pause*)

EUGENE: Milo!

(*Jocko and Milo enter*)

MILO: What?

EUGENE: She still wants to do it.

MILO: Okay. How do you want to set this up?

SKYE: Just stand there, I guess.

EUGENE: Milo!

MILO: Just be calm, Eugene. It'll all be over in a minute or two.

SKYE: You don't know that. Okay.

(*Eugene stands awkwardly. Skye throws a punch. He ducks; she continues throwing four more punches, backing him up. He continues to block the shots. She begins kicking him, but again he blocks her*)

JOCKO: I don't believe this.

SKYE: No blocking!!

EUGENE: Whadda you mean?

SKYE: No blocking or you rot in jail for twenty years!

MILO: You'll have to put your arms down, Eugene.

JOCKO: You want us to hold him for you, Skye?

SKYE: Let's see if it's necessary.

EUGENE: What are you helping her for? I thought we were supposed to be friends!

SKYE: Yeah, you better.

(*They hold his arms. Skye gets set; she brushes back his hair, takes aim, and squeezes his cheeks very hard. He yells. She grabs his ear and twists it painfully. Bart, hearing the noises, enters with a beer bottle [Break away]*)

BART: What's this?

(*Skye pinches him in the stomach a few times, each time Eugene lets out painful noises. She then prepares to punch him by winding up, but instead she kicks him in the groin. He doubles over; she turns him around by the ears, winds up, and punches him right in the mouth. Eugene goes down. Skye goes after him, kicks him on the back of the leg, stomps on his foot, and kicks him twice in the butt. He tries crawling away, but she kicks him once again, this time in the stomach. He tries to get to his knees, but she winds up and punches him in the face again. This time the punch not only drops Eugene but Skye is in pain too*)

JOCKO: Keep your thumbs on the outside.

MILO: Is that it?

SKYE: Oh no.

(*Eugene gets up, staggering*)

SKYE: Just a minute. Grab him.

(*As Milo and Jocko grab Eugene, Skye takes off her blouse*)

SKYE: Get me a cup of coffee, okay, my friend? Do you like Ping-Pong? I like to play the game, but not to watch it much! My friend!

(*Skye, using two hands interlocked, hits him across the face, then in the stomach. He falls to his knees. She hits him with a beer bottle and sends him to dreamland. She stands over him for a second, making sure she has finished*)

SKYE: I'm all packed. (*She puts on her blouse*)

MILO: Is *that* it?

SKYE: Yup.

JOCKO: This is amazing.

(*Milo takes out the release. Skye signs it*)

SKYE: Jocko, you want to witness this?

JOCKO: Sure. Feel better?

SKYE: Like a champ.

MILO: Are you sure you don't want to work for my legal department?

(*Skye exits into her room. Bart, who exited into his room after the fight, enters with his Polaroid. He crosses to Eugene and takes a few shots*)

JOCKO: Why did you let her do it?

MILO: She was right. And just maybe he won't do it again.

(*Milo and Jocko pick up Eugene and drag him into his room. Bart snaps one more outside Eugene's room*)

JOCKO: How many fingers I got up?

(*Milo and Jocko exit with Eugene. Skye enters with her bags*)

SKYE: How's he doing?

BART: He doesn't look as bad as you do, dear.

SKYE: Wait'll tomorrow.

(*Skye exits into her room for the rest of her bags. Jocko enters and Skye re-enters. Milo enters*)

SKYE: Oh, Jocko, remember that phone number I gave you last night?

JOCKO: Yeah . . .

SKYE: Don't forget to call me, okay?

JOCKO: (*Stunned*) Sure.

SKYE: Better still, why don't you come with me?

JOCKO: What?

SKYE: Come back to the States with me. Be my assistant.

JOCKO: Be your assistant?

SKYE: Yup.

JOCKO: Why me?

SKYE: You're very impressive. You don't think you are, but you are.

JOCKO: I'm busy. Ask him.

SKYE: Him? I don't want him. He's a mogul. Moguls are a dime a dozen for girls like me. With moguls, after you spend one night in their house and they show you all their possessions, they're real boring. But you—you could keep me entertained for hours!

JOCKO: Entertained? With what?

SKYE: With talk. With opinions. I don't know anybody who cares about the stuff you care about. The rhyme scheme of limericks . . . the laziness of photographs. You'd really keep me on my toes.

JOCKO: I've got a job here.

SKYE: How do you know Dave Hawk isn't waiting at the Manila airport right this minute?

MILO: Dave Hawk?

JOCKO: Milo, am I going to get fired?

MILO: Who said anything about getting fired?

SKYE: You're so naive. When this thing comes out—and it will, I believe him—he's the one who'll get all the credit, not you.

JOCKO: Oh, I don't know.

SKYE: Jocko, this man has an ego the size of Alaska! *Parabola of Death* won't be about the war in Angola or somebody's racial consciousness; it'll be about *him*. Don't you see that?

(*Milo laughs in appreciation*)

SKYE: You don't have any idea who you are or what you can become, but I do. God, with me around you could have lots of accomplishments.

JOCKO: What would I be your assistant to?

SKYE: Didn't you hear him? I could be president of Paramount! Except I'm beginning to think that's a dumb job, too.

JOCKO: You're serious.

SKYE: You're not meant for this wheeling, dealing business; I am. You're meant to be protected and coddled so you can write down sensitive thoughts or make pottery. And you're certainly not meant to be celibate. That's one condition: you can't come and live in my house on Wonderland Avenue unless we have sex.

JOCKO: But I don't want to live in your house on Wonderland Avenue whether we have sex or not!

SKYE: Don't worry—I'm not all that demanding anymore. I mean, I don't care about teenage boys like every other dumb woman my age. I'm slowing down.

JOCKO: I don't believe it. How long do you have in mind?

SKYE: As long as it feels good.

JOCKO: That's too long.

SKYE: Well, how about three days? You want to leave after three days, go ahead.

JOCKO: You want me to give up the most artistically rewarding job I've ever had to go live with you for three days in a city I cannot bear?

SKYE: Oh, come on, Jocko—I'll protect you from mean old L.A. I'll save you from the Nixon Freeway and sculptable air. You'll love it! Come on, what do you say?

MILO: Yeah, what do you say?

JOCKO: No, it's too crazy.

SKYE: (*Exhausted*) Okay. Well, call me when and if you ever finish shooting this bomb.

MILO: Is that it?

SKYE: (*Putting on sunglasses*) Yeah, that's it, I guess.

MILO: Well, go get in the helicopter, Skye. I'll be there in a second.

(*Skye exits with her bags*)

JOCKO: I feel as though I've just been through another typhoon.

MILO: The world has not heard the last of that one. All right. I've got a picture to finish.

JOCKO: And I've got an ending for you.

MILO: You do? What is it?

JOCKO: At the last bunker, see, O'Hara, surrounded by the beat-up remains of his once gaudy band of mercenaries, looks over their wounded, battered forms, climbs to the ridge of the hill and stares down at a thousand pitch-black African faces spread out like an ocean before him. He realizes what his life has been, rises to his full height, and just before they spatter him with a torrent of machine gun bullets, he yells into their midst, "NIIIIIIGGGGGGGEEEEEEEERRR!!" and . . . and . . . and . . . dies.

MILO: (*After a pause*) Very interesting, Jocko. I like it. I gotta pee. Does this bathroom work?

JOCKO: Yeah.

(*Milo exits into the bathroom*)

JOCKO: He likes it! He likes it! How can he like it? It's ridiculous. He can't like it. *I* don't like it. What am I doing here? (*He exits into his room. After a pause, he comes running out with his luggage, exiting up left*) How bad can three days be?

(*Jocko is gone. Bart enters from his room. He crosses up to the table, looking for a match. A toilet flushes. Milo enters*)

MILO: Where's Jocko? (*He looks into Jocko's room*)

BART: (*Looking out the window*) He's running to your helicopter with his bags.

MILO: (*Crossing up to the window*) With his bags! (*Into walkie-talkie*) Killer Joe, Killer Joe, this is Milo, over.

KILLER JOE: (*Voice only*) Go ahead Milo, over.

MILO: Did Dave Hawk's plane land yet?

KILLER JOE: (*Voice only*) Roger, over.

MILO: Good. Tell him to come straight to my house. I'll be back in Manila in forty-five minutes. Over and out. (*To Bart*) There'll be a production meeting this afternoon at three o'clock. I'll need a list of your equipment damage. (*He exits*)

BART: Yes, sir. Winston! Winston!

(*Winston enters with a huge breakfast for Bart*)

WINSTON: Bart, your breakfast.

BART: (*Getting two beers*) Come on in here, Winston my boy. Sit down and have a beer, on me.

(*Winston sits reluctantly. Bart notices his discomfort*)

BART: Awww, don't worry about that shelf, Winston. Happens to the best of us. You know what you did? You made dog! Best damn dog I've had since '67 working for Sir Run-Run Shaw in Taiwan.

WINSTON: Thank you, Bart. Your beard?

BART: That's nothing. I can grow that back in a week. That's what I like about hair—it works while you sleep. Papa loved dog. "And the dog was good. And the

N04

difference between this dog and the wild dog of the pack was that this dog knew his mortality and the wild dog didn't." Eh? Drink up my friend. You shoulda seen Taiwan in '67. We were making one of those imitation Bruce Lee karate movies, you know? *Bamboo Heart Punch.* God, they had me jumpin'—four and five wounds a day. (*The lights start to fade*) I had one wound called the eyeball jerk—you shoulda seen it! Two split chests, a cauterized stump, compound fractures . . . Blood everywhere!

THE END